The Potter Pensieve

Trivial Delights from the World of
HARRY POTTER

Published by
Arcane ®
an imprint and registered trade mark of Bobcat Books Limited,
8/9 Frith Street, London W1D 3JB, UK.

Cover illustration by Hannah Firmin courtesy of Duncan Baird Publishers Ltd.
Jacket design by Tara O'Leary.
Order No. SMB1023
ISBN: 1-86074-654-3

Every effort has been made to trace the copyright holders of the photographs
in this book but one or two were unreachable. We would be grateful if the
photographers concerned would contact us.

Printed in the United Kingdom.

A catalogue record for this book is available from the British Library.

www.musicsales.com

The Potter Pensieve

Trivial Delights from the World of
HARRY POTTER

Karen Farrington
and Lewis Constable

arcane

— WHAT IS A PENSIEVE? —

A pensieve is a shallow stone basin decorated with runes and other ancient symbols that glows from within, and Harry initially encounters one in *Harry Potter And The Goblet Of Fire* in Professor Dumbledore's office. Dumbledore explains its purpose: 'One simply siphons the excess thoughts from one's mind, pours them into the basin and examines them at one's leisure. It becomes easier to spot patterns and links, you understand, when they are in this form.' In the wizarding world, users put a wand to their temple to transfer their inner thoughts from the head to the pensieve or a container. These thoughts materialise as silvery or pearly gaseous strands that swirl in multi-colours.

The name for this useful implement of Dumbledore's probably derives from the word 'pensive' (ie thoughtful), or perhaps it comes from a combination of the French verb *penser* (to think, itself a root of the term 'pensive') and the word 'sieve', representing an object with a fine mesh used in cooking and in the garden to sift out the useless dirt from the useful particles.

If you've ever had thoughts about Harry Potter while you've been reading the books or watching the films, you'll most likely find them written here in this book, explored, expanded and coupled with the answers you are seeking. Dancing enquiries that leap from the pages have all been drawn together here. To read it is to satisfy an unspoken curiosity about the Potter world, the legends attached to it and the facts that anchor it to our own Muggle existence.

— MINISTRY OF MAGIC —

Cornelius Fudge is the self-important and small-minded one-time Minister for Magic. He is short in height, instinct and insight and was always anxious that Dumbledore was after his job. Like any ministry, there's an array of departments at the Ministry of Magic, each with its own head, but they all ultimately fall into the corral run by Fudge and his successors. Here's a swift run-down of the departments that are housed in the multi-layered ministry hidden in the heart of London.

DEPARTMENT OF MAGICAL LAW ENFORCEMENT
This department's responsibility is to make sure witches and wizards toe the line, although its effect in countering Voldemort has not been noticeably huge. Located on the second level of the Ministry, it is like a police and justice department combined. Among its sub-departments are the Improper Use of Magic Office, Misuse of Muggle Artefacts Office (run by Arthur Weasley, who is constantly campaigning against the mistreatment of Muggles), Auror HQ (concerned with the capture of Death Eaters) and the Wizengamot Administration Services (the equivalent of the High Court). The department's high-flying head, Amelia Bones, has a niece at Hogwarts in Harry's year.

DEPARTMENT FOR MAGICAL ACCIDENTS AND CATASTROPHES
This department remedies the disasters wrought with mad magic. Among its departments are the Accidental Magic Reversal Squad, which orchestrates cover-ups to hide magical mistakes from Muggles; Obliviator HQ, which wipes the memories of Muggles who have witnessed inappropriate events (similar to that carried out by Will Smith and Tommy Lee Jones in *Men In Black*); the Muggle-worthy Excuse Committee, which is responsible for sorting out credible explanations for magic; and the Committee on Experimental Charms.

DEPARTMENT FOR THE REGULATION AND CONTROL OF MAGICAL CREATURES
Led by Amos Diggory, this fourth-level department incorporates the Goblin Liaison Office and the Pest Advisory Bureau, and it also splits into Beast, Being and Spirit Divisions. In the Beast division there is the non-functioning Centaur Liaison Office (non-functioning because of the isolationist stance taken by centaurs), the Dragon Research and Restraint Bureau, the Ghoul Task Force, the Werewolf Registry and the Werewolf Capture Unit. Also part of this department is the now-infamous Committee for the Disposal of Dangerous Creatures, headed by the decidedly dodgy Walden Macnair.

DEPARTMENT OF INTERNATIONAL MAGICAL CO-OPERATION
It's always a hard task to keep nations united, but that's the job of this department, once led by Barty Crouch, Sr. It includes the International Magical

Trading Standards Body, the International Magic Office of Law and the International Confederation of Wizards.

DEPARTMENT OF MAGICAL TRANSPORT

This department's area of responsibility is the ways in which wizards travel between venues, and standing under its umbrella is the Floo Network Authority; Broom Regulatory Control; the Portkey Office, which designates suitable portkeys; and the Apparation Test Centre, which certifies adult apparators.

DEPARTMENT OF MAGICAL GAMES AND SPORTS

Keeping the wizarding world fit through sport, this department is primarily concerned with Quidditch. Indeed, the British and Irish Quidditch League HQ is based within it, although it is also involved with the Official Gobstones Club and the Ludicrous Patents Office. Ludo Bagman, the accomplished Quidditch player and committed gambler, was once to be found in this seventh-level office.

DEPARTMENT OF MYSTERIES

It's good to know that there are still some conundrums that defy even wizard wisdom and must be scrutinised accordingly! Prophecies are also safeguarded here. It's a spooky place, though, and must be entered with care.

— WITCH DATE 1 —

In 1612 there was a rebellion among goblins, who were perhaps unsettled by strange events unfolding in the Muggle world. This was the year of the Pendle witch trials in Lancashire, after which ten people were hanged. In addition, one woman died in gaol and another was hanged across the border in Yorkshire for witchcraft while a third was cleared of murder and sentenced to a year behind bars. It was, quite simply, the most sensational trial of the era, with accusations of murder by witchcraft, embellished by personal confession, being levelled across the country, although in truth the trials appeared to revolve around a feud between two families. What's most curious, however, is the detail freely given by the accused, who were apparently not tortured, simply informative. Also curiously, the home of one family was Malkin Tower, which perhaps provides a distant link to Harry Potter's Madam Malkin. The backdrop to the drama was a national hysteria – backed wholeheartedly by King James I – about the presence of witches in society and their activities.

— POPULAR PRISONER —

An ongoing online poll taken by *The Scotsman* newspaper compiled from votes cast via a website has aimed to settle a long-running dispute among Potter fans by determining once and for all which is the most popular Harry Potter book, out of the first five adventures. The results at the start of 2005 stood like this:

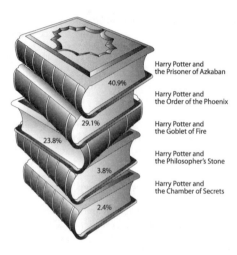

Harry Potter and
the Prisoner of Azkaban

Harry Potter and
the Order of the Phoenix

Harry Potter and
the Goblet of Fire

Harry Potter and
the Philosopher's Stone

Harry Potter and
the Chamber of Secrets

The total number of votes cast at the time was 7,268.

— POTTERING ON THE INTERNET —

According to MSN's internet search engine, Harry Potter was the most popular literary figure sought by British web-users in 2004. Even so, it's slightly humiliating for a famous wizard to be beaten overall by a Barbie doll. Here's the full Top 20 of most requested words and phrases:

1 Big Brother
2 Inland Revenue
3 Horoscopes
4 EastEnders
5 Football

— WHAT'S IN A NAME? 1 —

In *Harry Potter And The Goblet Of Fire*, Harry stuffs gillyweed into his mouth to enable him to breathe underwater without special apparatus. Curiously, when a number of teachers enjoy a drink at Madam Rosmerta's in *Harry Potter And The Prisoner Of Azkaban*, Professor McGonagall has a gillywater. It's unlikely, however, that the two are related. A gill is, of course, an organ that fish have which enables them to breathe underwater, and it's also the term that describes part of a mushroom or toadstool. Also, gill ale is beer with an infusion of ground ivy, and it's likely that this is the professor's tipple of choice. It's possible that a little bit of joined-up thinking by JK Rowling might well have linked the weed with the beverage.

— GAME LANE —

An ordinary street in Cambourne, Cambridgeshire, has come to prominence due to its extraordinary name. And, although there's no evidence of nightly broomstick duels, the homes of Quidditch Lane have recently begun to evoke the Harry Potter world, with house names including 'The Snitch' and 'The Quaffle'. In fact, Quidditch Lane was in existence long before the publication of the Harry Potter books, its name deriving from a long-standing term for a dry ditch rather than a literary phenomenon.

— WIZARD SHOPS —

Apothecary (name unknown)	spell ingredients outlet	Diagon Alley
Borgin & Burkes	dark arts shop	Knockturn Alley
Cauldron shop (name unknown)		Diagon Alley
Dervish & Banges	novelty shop	Hogsmeade
Eeylops' Owl Emporium		Diagon Alley
Florean Fortescue's	ice-cream parlour	Diagon Alley
Flourish and Blotts	bookshop	Diagon Alley
Gambol and Japes	wizarding joke shop	Diagon Alley
Gladrags Wizardwear	outfitters	Hogsmeade
Gringotts	bank	Diagon Alley
The Hog's Head	public house	Hogsmeade
Honeydukes	sweetshop	Hogsmeade
The Leaky Cauldron	public house	Charing Cross Road, London
Madam Malkin's Robes for All Occasions	robe shop	Diagon Alley
Madam Puddifoot's tea shop		Hogsmeade
Magical Menagerie	pet shop	Diagon Alley
Obscurus Books	publishers	Diagon Alley
Ollivander's	makers of fine wands since 382 BC	Diagon Alley
Owl Post Office		Hogsmeade
Purge & Dowse Ltd	empty shop that's the façade for St Mungo's	London
Quality Quidditch Supplies	sports shop	Diagon Alley
Scrivenshaft's Quill Shop	purveyors of writing implements	Hogsmeade
Three Broomsticks	public house	Hogsmeade
Twilfitt & Tatting's	robe shop	unknown
Weasleys' Wizard Wheezes		Diagon Alley

Whizz Hard Books	publishers	Diagon Alley
Zonko's Wizard Joke Shop		Hogsmeade

— MUGGLE ITEMS THAT WOULD FASCINATE — ARTHUR WEASLEY

- iPod
- Solar-powered anything
- Torches
- Late-running trains
- Digital watches that only tell the time rather than giving essential information, such as if someone is in trouble
- Firelighters
- Fire extinguishers
- Firemen
- Euros
- Parking meters
- Remote-controlled aeroplanes
- Rubik's cube
- Aircraft, particularly the technology behind keeping them airborne

— INDIAN CHARM —

Two days after its release, *Harry Potter And The Half-Blood Prince* had notched up sales of more than 100,000 in Mumbai, India, which is surprising because fakers had already flooded the streets with pirated copies of the book, selling at less than a third of the official cover price. The illicit copies were available less than two days after the book's launch. Mumbai is famous for the skilled workmanship of its rip-off merchants, and most popular movies, music albums and software have been pirated there.

— MAGIC NUMBERS —

Did you notice that the telephone number dialled to gain entry into the Ministry of Magic – 6-2-4-4-2 – spells 'magic' on telephone keypads?

— HOUSE ELF HISTORY —

Having a house elf at your disposal might seem like a dream come true, giving you someone to pick up your clothes from the bedroom floor, prepare meals and clean up afterwards, and generally someone who will slave away without wishing for a reward, either financial or in kind.

When she finds out about the existence of house elves, Hermione is instantly uncomfortable with the exploitation that goes on with those little guys. Perhaps you feel you could keep a house elf and a clear conscience at the same time, but consider this: the house elves we get to know well in the Harry Potter series are all seriously flawed. Do you think you could endure the attentions of Dobby for more than a day? Loyal and loving though he is, there's a complete lack of self-control there. His friend Winky gets hooked on Butterbeer and her dependency is tragic to behold. Hokey seems the most reliable of the bunch, although we don't get to know much about him.

Worst of all, you could get a Kreacher, the house elf devoted to the horrid Blacks. Ultimately, Harry is saddled with him but, wisely, never trusts him.

— WITCH DATE 2 —

Newt Scamander tells us that the International Confederation of Wizards had a famous summit meeting in 1692, ostensibly to discuss the number of magical creatures to be hidden from Muggle view. The meeting went on for seven weeks and the selection of beings and beasts that would thereafter be considered mythical by the Muggle population dominated the agenda.

However, it's likely that the Salem witch trials were also discussed, as they occurred in that same year. The events unfolded in Salem village, a small community in a Massachusetts Bay colony repressed by the Puritan faith, rivalry with other localities and fear of American Indian attack.

It all began when a group of children grew hysterical after hearing the eerie stories of a slave woman named Tituba, who was presumably recounting a version of some ancient tales from her home of Barbados. Ultimately, the diagnosis of the local doctor was that the children were bewitched. In their highly charged emotional state, the youngsters then accused various adults of indulging in witchcraft, and these unfortunates were then swiftly arrested and interrogated. The punishment for witchcraft in that era was death.

When they realised that adults were hanging on their every word, the children continued with their accusations, growing ever more outlandish in their claims.

Things quickly got out of hand. From the trial notes, it appears that one of the accused 'fell down and tumbled about like a Hog', while a woman was said to be perched on a beam in the courtroom ceiling, nurturing a yellow bird between her fingers. Everyone got so caught up with the scandal that they would believe anything.

One deputy constable, John Willard, was executed when he refused to make more arrests at the behest of the children. Two dogs were found guilty of witchcraft and were killed. A further 18 people – four of them men – were hanged on Gallows Hill in 1692, while another man was pressed to death, with heavy stones piled on his outstretched body because he refused to make a plea of innocent or guilty at his trial, preventing the hearing from going ahead. In all, some 150 people were penned in local prisons during the episode, at a time when prison conditions were woeful. Among the outrages was the treatment of five-year-old Dorcas Good, who was chained to the wall of a prison dungeon for more than seven months.

The subtext to all this was the personal ambitions of Increase and Cotton Mather, two learned clerics who manipulated events to their own ends, not least to prove their enduring beliefs that witches really existed and were a grave threat to society. They also wished to discredit a particular cleric associated with Salem, namely Reverend George Burroughs, and so helped to perpetuate the frenzy.

At Burroughs' execution, Cotton Mather addressed the crowds, according to the account published by Robert Calef in 1700 'partly to declare that [Burroughs] was no ordained minister and partly to possess the People of his guilt, saying that the Devil has often been transformed into an Angel of Light; and this did somewhat appease the People and the Executions went on.'

— WITCH DATE 2 (CONT'D) —

The people of Salem grew weary of the rabid persecutions, however, and began to realise that they'd been blinded by a curious mixture of fantasy and hysteria that might well have been a response to the fierce restrictions imposed on them by their Puritan lifestyle. The first arrests were made on 1 March and the final hanging took place on 22 September.

Meanwhile, back at the wizards' summit, it was decided that 28 species of beast, including dragons, should be obscured from human sight.

— THE SAME BUT DIFFERENT —

As the Harry Potter series came under increased scrutiny, there were inevitably comparisons drawn between the schoolboy wizard and Luke Skywalker, the hero of the 1980s blockbuster film series Star Wars. Author JK Rowling insists that the twist in her tale will not mimic that of George Lucas's sci-fi series, but nevertheless there are some similarities, not least the issues of prophecy and destiny that each hero must unravel. Here's a quick comparison between the two:

HARRY POTTER SERIES
HERO: Harry Potter, raised by an uncle and aunt
CREATED BY: JK Rowling
GROWING UP: Unaware of magical powers in childhood until contact with Hagrid
PALS: Ron and Hermione
SAGE: Dumbledore – old and wise
VILLAIN: Lord Voldemort, who favours black clothing
CREATIVE CREATURES: Buckbeak the Hippogriff, Dobby the house elf, Thestrals, Blast-Ended Skrewts
THE STORY SO FAR: Harry Potter books I–VI
FILMS: *Harry Potter And The Philosopher's Stone* (2001)
Harry Potter And The Chamber Of Secrets (2002)
Harry Potter And The Prisoner Of Azkaban (2004)
Harry Potter And The Goblet Of Fire (2005)

STAR WARS SERIES
HERO: Luke Skywalker, raised by an aunt and uncle
CREATED BY: George Lucas
GROWING UP: Unaware of Jedi powers until contact with Obi-Wan Kenobi

PALS: Han Solo and Princess Leia

SAGE: Yoda – old, wizened and wise

VILLAIN: Emperor Palpatine, who favours black garb

CREATIVE CREATURES: Chewbacca the wookie, C3PO, R2-D2, Ewoks, Jabba the Hutt

THE STORY SO FAR: Books exist, and there are many on the theme of the Expanded Universe, but really it's all about the films, listed as per the storyline order listed below:

Episode I: The Phantom Menace (1999)

Episode II: Attack Of The Clones (2002)

Episode III: Revenge Of The Sith (2005)

Episode IV: A New Hope (1977)

Episode V: The Empire Strikes Back (1980)

Episode VI: Return Of The Jedi (1983)

— ANOTHER HARRY POTTER —

As the world went wild about Harry, unexpected fame was brought to a hitherto-forgotten grave that has since been transformed into a shrine by tributes from wizard fans. The grave belongs to another Harry Potter, an 18-year-old with the Worcestershire Regiment, who was among the British forces sent to quell insurgents in Palestine shortly before the outbreak of the Second World War. He died on 22 July 1939 in Hebron, probably the victim of a sniper's bullet. His grave in the Commonwealth War Graves Commission cemetery in Ramla, near Tel Aviv, lay in obscurity for more than half a century until sharp-eyed fans noticed the name link with the world's latest literary phenomenon and began lavishing attention on it.

Now it is known that Harry Potter the soldier lied about his age to join up at 16 in 1937. Before his career in the army, he left school at 14 and fixed roller skates before starting work in a carpet factory. He was one of eight children living in a small house in Kidderminster, and his father – a First World War veteran – worked as a cobbler. Relatives are delighted that his distant grave is being cared for. As for the local town, its burghers have included the grave on its tourist trail and invited members of Potter's family to visit. For the record, he is one of several Harry Potters in English history.

— WIZARD SWEETS —

For the pupils at Hogwarts, there's a fine array of goodies to satisfy any sweet tooth. Here's a list of wizard sweets and, where relevant, their magic effects.

Chocolate frogs – A firm favourite with everyone, these enchanted frogs may hop, and at Christmas it's not unusual to receive a box of them as a present. More significantly, each box comes with a collectors' card featuring a (moving) picture and description of a famous witch or wizard.

Fizzing whizzbees – Delicious sweet with an exciting side-effect: they make you hover a couple of inches above the ground.

Drooble's best blowing gum – Enables the consumer to blow bubbles the size of a room that last for days.

Fudge flies – Not for the queasy.

Sherbet lemons – An old perennial from our grannies' era, these sweets remain a hit in both Muggle and wizarding worlds. They're one of Dumbledore's favourites.

Cockroach cluster – Uncomfortably crunchy.

Jelly slugs – Don't eat them outdoors in case you swallow the real thing in error.

Nougat – Another old-style sweet, popular in the East.

Black-pepper imps – Leave you smoking at the mouth.

Tooth-flossing string mints – Sweets that are ostensibly good for your teeth.

Ice mice – Make your teeth squeak.

Peppermint toads – Best remembered for their ability to hop inside the stomach.

Sugar quills – Ideal as a surreptitious snack during class.

Exploding bon-bons – Eat one if you dare.

Bertie Bott's every-flavour bean – Beware of ear wax, bogey and tripe flavours.

Blood lollipops – Primarily for vampires.

Mint humbugs – To be found in Hagrid's coat pockets, although there's no indication as to whether they are magical or standard.

Golden toffees

Coconut ice – Try making it at home.

Acid pops – Responsible for burning a hole through Ron's tongue when he was aged seven.

Chocoballs – Filled with strawberry mousse and clotted cream, these sweets are a dieter's nightmare.

Toffee eclairs – Another sweet to which Dumbledore is partial. It's amazing he has any teeth at all.

Crystallised pineapple – Horace Slughorn's favourite treat.

— FAB FILM —

Seven months after its release, *Harry Potter And The Prisoner Of Azkaban* was number one in the Yahoo! Movies chart of the best films of 2004, judged in terms of overall popularity. Harry beat off some stiff opposition to claim the top spot. The top ten went like this:

10. *Resident Evil: Apocalypse*
9. *The Grudge*
8. *The Incredibles*
7. *Van Helsing*
6. *Shrek 2*
5. *Mean Girls*
4. *The Passion Of The Christ*
3. *Spider-Man 2*
2. *Troy*
1. *Harry Potter And The Prisoner Of Azkaban*

— BOARDING-SCHOOL BOOKS THROUGH THE AGES —

Nicholas Nickleby by Charles Dickens (1812–70)
Tom Brown's Schooldays by Thomas Hughes (1822–96)
Stalky & Co by Rudyard Kipling (1865–1936)
Billy Bunter by Frank Richards (1876–1961)
Mallory Towers series by Enid Blyton (1897–1968)
St Claire's series by Enid Blyton
Goodbye Mr Chips by James Hilton (1900–54)
Jennings by Anthony Buckeridge (1912–2004)
The Prime Of Miss Jean Brodie by Dame Muriel Spark (1912–)
St Trinian's series by Ronald Searle (1920–)

— WIZARD HOLIDAY DESTINATIONS —

EGYPT

A holiday destination for the Weasley family and thousands of others who enjoy roasting weather and the warm waters of the Red and Mediterranean Seas, Egypt is the most populated of all the north African countries. It is cut through by both the Nile River and Suez Canal and has become a cultural beacon for the region, but perhaps it's most famous for its ancient history, evidence of which can be seen in the pyramids, the sphinx, the temple at Karnak and the Valley of the Kings, where the treasures of Tutenkhamen's tomb were uncovered. Egypt measures its history in millennia, and it has a rich mythology. Its flag takes the form of horizontal stripes of red, white and black, with the Egyptian coat of arms embedded in the central stripe.

TRANSYLVANIA

Tucked away in central Europe, Transylvania (literally 'beyond the forest' in Latin) is notorious in the wizarding world for its lively dragon population and the fact that its head of Magical Co-operation refused to sign the International Ban on Duelling. It's an exciting place for a holiday, you might think, especially given the fact that its Quidditch team resoundingly beat Britain's by 390 points to 10. In fact, Transylvania is more a region than a country, marked out by mountains in Romania and stretching out towards Hungary, Serbia and the Ukraine. Transylvania was put on the map by perhaps its most famous inhabitant, Vlad the Impaler, a pretty dreadful fellow who, as his name implies, thought up some dire punishments for his enemies. It was his reputation that gave rise to the legend of the vampire Dracula.

BULGARIA

This is a top-ranking holiday destination for most Quidditch fans. The main aim for visitors here is to play on the same hallowed turf above which the world-championship finalists compete, perchance where heroes like Viktor Krum once flew. There might also be the added bonus of meeting a Veela, the captivating national mascots. Muggles could do a lot worse than holiday in Bulgaria, a country whose mountains provide fine winter skiing, while there are some top-notch summer resorts on the Black Sea, as well as the spectacular if slightly polluted Danube River. Bulgaria is becoming the surprise choice for numerous second-home owners around Europe.

IRELAND

This is another nation that's close to the heart of the Quidditch fan, particularly given its success in the World Cup, yet there's much more to Ireland than bludgers and broomsticks. Formally named Eire, Ireland lies to the west of Britain and is about a third of its size. Golf, fishing, cycling and drinking Guinness are all popular pastimes for its residents and holidaymakers alike. The good news is that it's known as 'the emerald isle' because the grass there is so brilliantly green, but the bad news is that this is because it rains for such a lot of the time, summer and winter, especially in the west.

ALBANIA

Bertha Jorkins picked Albania as a holiday destination, and it proved an unfortunate choice, given that Voldemort also plumped to go there. Still, there's a lot going for little Albania, hemmed in on the coasts of the Adriatic and Ionian Seas by Greece, Montenegro, and Macedonia and Serbia. The country boasts charming citrus orchards, olive groves and vineyards, and it has a delightfully dated feel, as a long period spent in isolation thanks to its Communist politics effectively set it apart from the rest of Europe. Albania is also distinguished in having two of the most oddly named leaders of the 20th century: King Zog I and Enver Hoxha.

LUXEMBOURG

This tiny European country made sporting headlines when its Quidditch team pretty much destroyed the Scotland side during a stunning World Cup campaign – astonishing when you consider that it measures just 51 miles (84km) in length, is only 32 miles (52km) wide and has a tiny population. Luxembourg is the world's only grand duchy, lying between Germany, France and Belgium, and it was a founder member of the European Community. While French and German is spoken there, the official language is Lëtzebuergesch. Bet you didn't know that!

— WIZARD HOLIDAY DESTINATIONS (CONT'D)—

UGANDA

The victor of a significant Quidditch clash with Wales, Uganda is currently enjoying an economic as well as a sporting revival. It was once a British possession, and its beauty prompted Winston Churchill to call it the 'pearl of Africa'. After it won independence, the country had a succession of unfortunate and at times ludicrous leaders who got up to all sorts of trickery and sent inflation to a level of 1,000 per cent. This is in the past, however, and the country, now on a much more stable footing, is beginning to appeal to tourists once again, much as its neighbour Kenya always has.

— OH, BABY —

In January 2005, JK Rowling gave birth to her third child, a baby girl, Mackenzie, to whom *Harry Potter And The Half-Blood Prince* is dedicated, as an 'ink and paper twin'. The name Mackenzie is most often used as a surname and is taken from the Gaelic *mac coinnich*, meaning 'good-looker'. Indeed, there is a Scottish clan by the name MacKenzie, whose motto is 'I shine but do not burn', and in Canada the Mackenzie River is named for explorer Sir Alexander Mackenzie (1764–1820), who made tracks across uncharted America in the last years of the 18th century. Perhaps the most famous person named Mackenzie, however, is actually a guy: Mackenzie Crook, who starred in the comedy series *The Office* and also in the film *Pirates Of The Caribbean: The Curse Of The Black Pearl*, among others.

— FOUR-POSTER BEDS —

Unlike most Muggle homes, Hogwarts rooms are furnished with four-poster beds, as is the Knight Bus. On such a bed, the mattress has a canopy supported by four posts at each corner and decked with curtains or drapes.

Today, four-poster beds seem the height of luxury, not least because of their mighty price tag. In fact, the first four-poster beds were designed with comfort and practicality in mind. Beds with roofs and curtains began to appear in Britain after the Norman Conquest and were originally designed to keep out the cold and rain blowing in through windows. (Remember, this was an era when doors were fitted only poorly and windows were covered by loose wooden shutters rather than glass, so it was crucial to keep out draughts.) Until then, most people slept on shelves recessed into the wall. When four-poster beds were introduced, the drapes had the added bonus of keeping insects and animals at bay. At this time the mattress would probably have been a linen sack stuffed with straw, sometimes topped with feather-filled pockets for added comfort.

— WITCH DATE 3 —

In 1750, a key clause was included in the International Statute of Wizarding Secrecy that has kept 'all magical beasts, beings and spirits' under wraps. It decreed that if any such creature came to the notice of the Muggle population, the local wizarding governing body would be brought before the International Confederation of Wizards to be punished.

In the same year, Westminster Bridge was opened in London and Jonas Hanway (1712–86) gained himself a reputation for using an umbrella during wet weather. (Previously, umbrellas had only ever been used by women.) Such was Hanway's devotion to the use of a brolly that this essential wet-weather shield was for a while known as a 'Hanway'. At that time, few more than a million people lived in America, and Britain's King George II was their monarch. Research has since shown that one penny in 1750 had greater purchasing power than £1 in the present-day UK.

— HOGWARTS VERSUS MIDDLE-EARTH —

Here's a brief comparison of how JK Rowling's heroes shape up to those in JRR Tolkien's The Lord Of The Rings trilogy.

	HOGWARTS	**MIDDLE-EARTH**
HERO **Character**	**HARRY POTTER** Quiet, shy, thoughtful, loner – sometimes low on confidence. Father's background means much is expected, adding to general angst. Loathes vengeance-seeking. Reluctant to have greatness thrust upon him. Bewildered in a bewildering world.	**FRODO BAGGINS** Ditto, except that uncle (Bilbo) is the relative with the big reputation.
Magical Powers	Impressive wand-smith whose magical abilities improve with age. By adolescence, has mastered spells way beyond his years (witness the Patronus created to repel the Dementors in *Harry Potter And The Prisoner Of Azkaban*).	Only one: a ring offering invisibility when worn among ordinary mortals. Unfortunately, it also attracts a nasty class of enemy: the Nazgûl.
Coping Skills	Not great. And not improved by regular reminders that his enemies want to kill him.	Gradually desert him. At his big moment, they vanish altogether.
Hobbies	Quidditch. Baiting Dudley Dursley.	Eating, drinking, eating, pipe-smoking and eating.
Plot: Bloggers' Guide	Geeky orphan brought up by bullying aunt and uncle discovers he's a wizard. Learns that two worlds co-exist on Earth with ordinary humans, or 'Muggles', unwittingly living alongside wizard folk. Sent to wizard boarding school to be taught magic.	Young hobbit* plucked from obscurity to lead quest aimed at destroying the Ring, an all-powerful chunk of magical bling-bling! Journeys through a fantastic world, accompanied by warriors, wizards and former drinking pals. Big battles

*Fat, diminutive fantasy creature with long fingers, hairy feet and a 'deep, fruity laugh'.

Destiny: To counter the dark wizard Voldemort.
Overall theme: Good versus evil. And don't write off the little guy.

amid seemingly hopeless causes.
Destiny: To overcome dark wizard Sauron.
Overall theme: Same as Harry's.

Where's It Happening?	In the UK, here and now. Specifically, at Hogwarts School (somewhere up north, probably Scotland), underneath and within central London. Also Privet Drive in the London suburb of Little Whinging.	In Middle-Earth, a magical world that existed long before our own. Action starts in the Shire (a rural idyll) and ends in Mordor (a dirty, evil, stinking, prison-like fortress that, unkind observers believe, might be modelled on the Welsh town of Wrexham).
Well 'ard Allies	Rubeus Hagrid; giant. Cheery disposition but fearful temper. Impresses opponents by tying their guns in knots. Don't mess with his pets. Things he might say: 'Tea'd be nice – 'less you've summat stronger?'	Gimli, son of Glóin; dwarf. Has definite anger-management issues. Over-competitive when slaughtering foes. Would be the archetypal mad axeman in any other book. Things he might say: 'Come and 'ave a go, if you think yer 'ard enough.'
Best Friends	Ron Weasley and Hermione Granger.	Sam(wise) Gamgee, Meri-adoc (Merry) Brandybuck and Peregrine (Pippin) Took.
Feathered Friends	Hedwig, an owl.	Gwaihir, the Windlord, greatest of all the Eagles of the North.
Horrid Bully And Unlikely Hero	Draco Malfoy and Neville Longbottom.	Saruman (a turncoat wizard) and Gollum (emaciated former hobbit-like creature tortured by addiction to the Ring).

— HOGWARTS VERSUS MIDDLE-EARTH (CONT'D) —

Power-crazed Baddie	Lord Voldemort (sometimes seen).	Sauron (rarely seen).
Strange Times	Wizards of the 1990s are locked in a 1950s time-warp of steam trains and Ford Anglia cars? Are they really that cautious about Muggle inventions? And if Arthur Weasley can drive from his home in Ottery St Catchpole to King's Cross Station – taking in at least one motorway and miles of congested London traffic – howcome he's baffled by bus stops?	Dark wizards such as Sauron and Saruman have invented gunpowder (that's how they blow up Helm's Deep), so why haven't they equipped their troops with pistols and rifles? It would soon stop all that sword-slashing and axe-wielding by the good guys, and a few machine guns would ensure Sauron conquered Middle-Earth in a couple of chapters. Ah, so *that's* why.
Handy To Have (Weapons/ Defences)	Ollivander wand made of holly wood and phoenix feather. ('Eleven inches, nice and supple.') A time-turner, which enables a user facing imminent death to nip back in time and do everything differently. (Maybe.) Invisibility cloak, which doesn't fool all wizards.	Sting, a magic sword that gleams when orcs approach. A shirt of *mithril* (mixture of silver and steel), virtually impenetrable chain mail. The Ring, which gives brief periods of invisibility, but don't wear it for too long.
What's The Worst That Could Happen?	Harry flunks his finals and drops out of Hogwarts, swapping his Quidditch kit and broom for a wetsuit and surfboard. Permanently chills out in a VW camper van parked at a beach in Newquay, Cornwall.	Frodo discovers he was wearing the wrong ring all along and everyone was just humouring him about being invisible. There's always one who takes the joke too far, though. Silly old Gollum!

— TREE-MENDOUS ACHIEVEMENT —

The Canadian version of *Harry Potter And The Order Of The Phoenix* is green. That is to say, it is printed on environmentally friendly, recycled paper. In producing the initial print run of 1 million books in this way, the printers prevented the destruction of 29,640 trees.

— STRAWBERRY AND PEANUT BUTTER ICE CREAM —

In *Harry Potter And The Chamber Of Secrets*, Harry, Hermione and Ron pass some time in Diagon Alley happily slurping on strawberry and peanut butter ice creams – not a flavour commonly found in Muggle parlours, but that's no reason to miss out. Here's a new recipe with which you too can create a bit of magic in your kitchen:

INGREDIENTS
One pint (568ml) whipping cream
11oz (311g) strawberries (specifically, two tins of strawberries, although frozen or fresh would also do. Be sure to mash them first.)
2oz (50g) icing sugar
3tbs (75g) crunchy peanut butter

Whip the cream until it's stiff. Add the other ingredients one at a time and mix each well until everything is thoroughly blended. Put the mixture in a plastic box and place in the freezer until it's almost hard. Then, simply tuck in! (Don't forget that cream products will keep no longer than two months in a freezer.)

— DREAM TEAM —

Have you ever wondered which is the best Quidditch team in the world? It could be Ron's favourite, the Chudleigh Cannons, or lesser known Japanese contender the Toyohashi Tengu. There's an argument to say that, nationally speaking, any member of the World Cup winning team from Ireland is in the frame. If you could make up a team of your own, a dream team with players culled from past years but picked at the peak of their form, who would it include? Here's a selection, humbly proposed as the best ever Quidditch VII:

- A keeper needs talent and attitude as well as a will to win, so this has to go to Oliver Wood, former Gryffindor captain and Hogwarts cup winner who is currently training with Puddlemere United reserve team. He's obviously got a great Quidditch-playing future ahead of him.

- In the first chaser position, the chosen candidate is Moran from Ireland, whose hands are so quick that you need a slo-mo replay to see if he has the quaffle or not.

- The second chaser position goes to Angelina Johnson, who has proved herself to be a fine shooter, even at her young age.

- Everybody hates him, but the third chaser spot goes to Marcus Flint, who deserves a place in the team mainly because he has the useful ability to link up play, and having a ruthless chaser on the team could help win matches.

- The first beater slot is earmarked for Ludo Bagman at the height of his playing prowess. Bagman appeared for England and the Wimbourne Wasps, so in his time he was among the greatest. (Now sadly gone to seed, he probably wouldn't stay on the pitch long these days for fear of being spotted by those to whom he owes money.)

- In the other beater position is Volkov, who has a short temperament and a mighty whack on the bludger that could unsettle a basilisk, never mind a chaser.

- In the seeker position – and this is the one you've all been waiting for – is Viktor Krum. I know, I know, he's too dark for most tastes and doesn't have the charm of our own Harry Potter. Indeed, he only just edged Harry out of this list, but the experience gained in playing for his country in the Quidditch World Cup outweighs Harry's talent, which has yet to be proven on the big stage.

— ILFRACOMBE SCARES —

According to Newt Scamander, a rogue Welsh green dragon caused havoc in 1932 by swooping among sunbathing Muggles at Ilfracombe, north Devon. The potentially dangerous situation was remedied by members of a wizarding family at the scene, who, having dispatched the beast, swiftly performed mass memory-loss charms to eradicate the shocking image from the populace's minds.

This colourful account is nothing more than the product of an over-fertile imagination, and it's about time the real truth of the Ilfracombe incident was told. In fact, the dragon took one look at Ilfracombe and its folk, let out an ear-piercing scream and, overwhelmed with horror, fled back across the Bristol Channel to Wales at speed. Speaking as an ex-pupil at the local comprehensive school, from which there are stunning views of the town, countryside and sea, this is, I can assure you, by far the most likely course of events.

Of course, this wasn't the first time that Ilfracombe people have frightened off unwelcome visitors. In 1797, when England and France were at war, a lone woman spotted some French ships prowling along the coast. With all the menfolk away fighting, she realised that the town was in peril. Undaunted, she rounded up some lady friends, and together they all marched to the top of the nearby cliffs with their red petticoats draped over their shoulders, beating a drum, looking from a distance every inch like a British regiment. Indeed, the French – not known for being far-sighted – thought that that was exactly what they were, and the cross-dressers won the day: the ships sailed on and the town was saved. (Today, Ilfracombe women are equally feisty, but, sad to note, fashion sense has not improved greatly in the region.)

Scamander goes on to say that one of the residents who escaped the effects of the memory-loss charm, known as 'Dodgy Dirk', maintained that a giant lizard in Ilfracombe punctured his lilo. I can confirm that select parts of Ilfracombe are teeming with dodgy characters who are actually more likely than any rampant reptile to put a pin in your lilo.

— AGE BEFORE BEAUTY —

At first glance, Arthur and Molly Weasley's offspring are a confusing mass of red-haired boys, anchored by a single girl. Just to clarify their names and ages, Bill, the oldest, is two years older than Charlie, who is three years older than Percy, who is two years older than the identical twins, Fred and George, who are again two years older than Ron, who is just a year older than Ginny. Geddit?

— WHO IS MERLIN? —

Everybody at Hogwarts has heard of Merlin, as he is among the elite on the Famous Witches and Wizards trading cards found in boxes of chocolate frogs. Even most Muggles can claim some knowledge of Merlin, as he has appeared in countless tales concerning King Arthur, round tables and swords apparently welded into stones.

But who was Merlin, really? Well, if he lived at all, Merlin was around in Britain during a period known as the Dark Ages, and the truth is that we know very little about what was going on back then. One of the architects of Merlin mythology was Geoffrey of Monmouth, writing in the 12th century, who noted events that allegedly happened more than 500 years earlier. No one knows how he came by this information.

The most enduring tale around Merlin is that he was the son of a nun who was made pregnant by an agent of the Devil. When he was baptised, Merlin lost any devilry in him but was left with magical powers.

Merlin is said to have forecast the killing of King Vortigern, who died during an ongoing spat between Saxons and Britons, while he is also credited with magically transporting massive stones from Wales or Ireland into an area now known as Salisbury Plain. The result was the magnificent Stonehenge.

Later, another king, Uther Pendragon, impregnated a rival's wife after subterfuge involving Merlin, and the result was King Arthur. Merlin became the boy's mentor, leaving his side only when the glorious kingdom Arthur wrought was shattered by infighting.

There are at least five different places in the UK that claim to be Merlin's burial site, which might suggest that there were two or more Merlins in existence in that shadowy world that unfolded before books were known.

— SPOT THE DIFFERENCE —

Nearly Headless Nick is a ghost while pesky Peeves is definitely a poltergeist. So how can you tell the two apart? It can be tricky for an amateur to distinguish one from the other, but there are some ways to tell distinguish them.

Poltergeists take their name from the German words *poltern* ('to knock') and *Geist* ('spirit'), because they're associated with loud, unexplained noises, including tapping, crashing and the slamming of doors. Ghosts, meanwhile, are sometimes prone to wailing, but they are more likely to be as silent as the grave.

In addition to being noisy, poltergeists might well emit foul smells, hide household items, interfere with electric lights or television reception and generally make a thorough nuisance of themselves by being disruptive and destructive. Ghosts, on the other hand, seem to be far less bumptious and intrusive by nature; other than giving you the shivers, they generally leave no evidence of their presence.

While ghosts are generally associated with dead people, poltergeists seem to be linked to the living. The most likely explanation to date for poltergeist activity is that it is caused by *psychokinesis*, a physical expression of a living person's mental energies, and a connection has indeed been made between poltergeist activity and the anxieties of nearby humans, generally teenage girls. Usually, such psychokinetic people are completely unaware of what's occurring.

Ghosts tend to lurk about in areas familiar to them, while poltergeists swing into action anytime, anywhere. However, while ghosts generally return to one place for years – even centuries – poltergeist activity tends to reach a crisis point and then generally disappears.

Also, ghosts are very often benign, which means that they wouldn't hurt a fly, while poltergeists are altogether more violent, hurling objects around rooms and sometimes causing injuries to the living. These extraordinary entities have also been linked to mystery pinches, bites and other threatening behaviour.

— FILM BLUNDERS —

Sharp-eyed fans have been swift to spot errors in the Harry Potter films. Incredibly, the number of blunders recorded on one internet site runs into scores for each of the movies, although not all reported fudges were 100 per cent convincing. However, we've selected some errors for you to watch out for next time you're viewing the blockbusters.

HARRY POTTER AND THE PHILOSOPHER'S STONE
- At the start of the film, Dumbledore magically dowses the street lamps in Privet Drive. In shots of the same area soon afterwards, there is no sign of street lighting.

- Before he goes into the great hall to be processed by the Sorting Hat, Ron's robes are open, then closed, then open again.

- At the feast marking the start of term, Harry is first sitting next to Ron when he goes to be selected for Gryffindor. When the food appears – oops! – he's sitting opposite Ron and next to Hermione.

- When Hagrid tows the Christmas tree into Hogwarts, his hair looks remarkably dry considering the snowy weather outside. In the next shot, though, when he's just a few paces ahead, his barnet is white with snow.

- When Hermione first cowers under the sinks in the Hogwarts toilets during the troll rampage, there are initially a few spots of water on the floor. In the next shot, the floor is soaked – and this before the troll fractures the water pipes.

HARRY POTTER AND THE CHAMBER OF SECRETS
- After the flying Ford Anglia crashes into the Whomping Willow, the front left light is clearly smashed. Moments later, the light is magically whole.

- When Errol the owl lets loose the howler, which lands in a bowl on the table, the seal is clearly broken. As Ron grabs the envelope, however, the seal is definitely whole.

- Harry hurts his arm while playing Quidditch, but as he watches the rogue bludger whizzing around the stadium he props himself up on both arms, apparently uninjured, before the next shot.

- When Moaning Myrtle makes an exit down the toilet bowl, there's a terrific splash – even though she's a ghost. Later, when she tries to hit Ron, he can't feel anything, so it's not clear whether she has enough about her to make a splash or not.

- After he's pushed into the Chamber of Secrets by Ron, Gilderoy Lockhart appears to fall vertically for a short spell before landing. Afterwards, Ron and Harry follow the same route but travel down a pipe like a slide for a far longer period of time.

HARRY POTTER AND THE PRISONER OF AZKABAN

- This is apparently a deliberate mistake, but in this film Hagrid's hut is in a completely different place than in the previous Harry Potter movies.

- When Snape finds Harry roaming the corridors at night, the confrontation is brief but intense. Curiously, the strings on Harry's hoodie adopt several different positions during the contretemps.

- When Hermione uses her time turner with Harry, it has a super-long chain. It's surprising that she doesn't trip over it when wearing it around her neck!

- When Hermione launches a stone into Hagrid's hut, it breaks a vase but leaves half of it standing. When the scene is replayed, following a few twists of the time turner, the vase breaks into small pieces and nothing is left standing.

- The clock is striking when Harry and Hermione go back in time. It strikes again as Fudge looks for the missing Buckbeak just minutes later. Has the Hogwarts clock gone haywire?

— ROUND ROOMS —

Dumbledore's room, guarded by gargoyles and atop a moving spiral staircase, is circular. This seems unusual today, when most domestic and commercial buildings have square or rectangular rooms, yet round rooms were once the norm, not only in grand castle towers but also in constructions as lowly as pigsties. The technique for building in a circle shape is known as *corbelling* and has been in use since prehistory. Many examples of ancient roundhouses still exist in France and Italy.

— IT'S IN THE STARS —

Although there's doubt about the year in which he was born, we know that Harry celebrates his birthday on 31 July, the same day as his creator, JK Rowling, was born. This means that the star sign shared by both character and author is Leo, one of 12 in the zodiac that allegedly governs personal characteristics. It seems likely that the predictions of published weekly horoscopes are little short of hogwash (for example, can one-twelfth of the population *really* anticipate good news from a mysterious stranger on any given day?), yet Harry shares many of the attributes that are commonly associated with his horoscope sign.

Leos are risk-takers who are honest, loyal, dignified, generous and shot through with a sense of responsibility. On the flip side, they tend towards stubbornness, can be cold-hearted if they've been hurt (something that Cho could vouch for) and are prone to sulking. Those born under Leo, a fire sign, enjoy glowing brightly at the centre of events with warmth and radiance, attracting the attention of others by doing so, and so they relish leadership. They're also sure to be sporty, enjoy family or party games and specialise in making great first impressions. Saturn moves into Leo on 16 July 2005 (the day on which, oddly, *Harry Potter And The Half-Blood Prince* was published), and according to astrologers this cosmic shift will bring challenges aplenty for Leos at a particularly sensitive time in their chart.

Lucky colours for Leos are yellow and orange, while their lucky flower is the blazing sunflower and their lucky metal is gold.

As part of a couple, a Leo is best suited to pairing with a Virgoan, Libran, Sagittarian, Arian, Gemini, Cancerian or another Leo. The relationships that suit them least tend to be with Capricorns and Pisceans.

Sharing a birthday with Harry (and, of course, JK Rowling) is actor Dean Cain, who starred in the TV series *Lois And Clark: The New Adventures Of Superman* between 1993 and 1997; actor Wesley Snipes, who played the title role in the Blade series of vampire action flicks; Australian tennis player Evonne Goolagong Cawley, who won the Australian Open four times and Wimbledon twice; actress Geraldine Chaplin; broadcaster Jonathan Dimbleby; and musician Jim Corr of The Corrs.

Hermione's birthday is 19 September, so she is a Virgo. This might explain why she's so addicted to schoolwork, as Virgoans are notoriously hard workers who quest for high standards. They also tend to be efficient, effective, logical and modest, but their biggest fault lies in their tendency to criticise or correct others. There's no doubt, though, that the astrological emphasis on analysis and organisation have helped Hermione out of scrapes in the past. Famous people who share Hermione's birthday include actor Kevin Zegers, comic Jimmy Fallon and actor Jeremy Irons, the voice of Scar in Disney's *The Lion King*.

For Virgoans, lucky colours are mustard, brown and cream, while their lucky flower is lavender and their lucky metal is mercury. Intriguingly, ideal partners for a Virgoan like Hermione include Leos like Harry, as well as Cancerians, Taureans, Capricorns, Scorpios and Librans. However, a relationship with a Piscean is going to be a difficult one – and guess what sign Ron is?

— IT'S IN THE STARS (CONT'D) —

With a birthday on 1 March, Ron is stoutly Piscean, which means he is compassionate, trusting and helpful. Yet Pisceans are prone to being sensationalist and blaming others for the predicaments in which they find themselves. Also, Pisceans can be tactless, self-pitying and may be unwilling to stand up for what they believe in. With those astrological influences, Ron was never going to be as staunch a prefect as Hermione. Pisceans get on best with other Pisceans, Arians, Taureans, Cancerians, Scorpios, Capricorns and Aquarians, although they risk a rocky relationship with Leos and Librans.

Famous people who were born on the same date as Ron include bandleader Glenn Miller, actor and director Ron Howard, actor Jensen Ackles of the TV series *Smallville* and singer Roger Daltrey.

— HOUSE ABOUT THAT? —

Hogwarts has four houses, each related to one of the school's founders, all of who lived centuries ago. Here's a swift guide to each house's rules:

GRYFFINDOR
NAMED AFTER: Godric Gryffindor
COLOURS: Scarlet and gold
ANIMAL EMBLEM: Lion

GHOST: Nearly Headless Nick
MOST COMPELLING ATTRIBUTE: Courage

HUFFLEPUFF
NAMED AFTER: Helga Hufflepuff
COLOURS: Yellow and black
ANIMAL EMBLEM: Badger
GHOST: The Fat Friar
MOST COMPELLING ATTRIBUTE: Steadfastness

RAVENCLAW
NAMED AFTER: Rowena Ravenclaw
COLOURS: Blue and silver
ANIMAL EMBLEM: Eagle
GHOST: The Grey Lady
MOST COMPELLING ATTRIBUTE: Intelligence

SLYTHERIN
NAMED AFTER: Salazar Slytherin
COLOURS: Green and silver
ANIMAL EMBLEM: Serpent
GHOST: The Bloody Baron
MOST COMPELLING ATTRIBUTE: Ambition

— CHEWING IT OVER —

Her desk is strewn with notes, books, pens and many screwed-up pieces of chewing-gum wrappers. That's because JK Rowling gave up smoking in 2000 and has used nicotine-flavoured gum to fend off the cravings for a cigarette ever since. Hooked since her schooldays, she's among 21 per cent of British women who are now ex-smokers. A further 25 per cent of the female population still indulges, however, despite the fact that 114,000 smokers in the UK die each year as a direct consequence of their habit. Perhaps even more galling, 450 children start smoking every day in the United Kingdom.

As campaigners against cigarettes (also known as 'cancer sticks') are quick to point out, tobacco is the only legally available consumer product that kills people when it is used entirely as intended.

— WHAT A ROTTER! —

The Harry Potter series has led to some serious literary study, which has been expounded in various worthy tomes (although we don't count this book among them!). However, it's also led to some serious amounts of fun in terms of mickey-taking. For instance, there was the Comic Relief spoof *Harry Potter And The Secret Chamberpot Of Azerbaijan*, performed on television in Britain to raise cash for those in need. There have also been books that parody the Harry Potter phenomenon, the most prominent of which have been written by Michael Gerber. A word of warning, however: they're definitely written for an adult market. So, just in case you don't get the opportunity to read it, here's a quick guide to Gerber's wizarding world, so you can compare it to the one you know and love.

Barry Trotter – Harry Potter
Lon Measley – Ron Weasley
Hogwash – Hogwarts
Ermine Cringer – Hermione Granger
Hafwid – Hagrid
Alpo Bumblemore – Albus Dumbledore
Muddle – Muggle
Nurse Pommefritte – Madam Pomfrey
Butterbourbon – Butterbeer
Lord Valumart – Lord Voldemort
Putresca Pufnstuf – Helga Hufflepuff
Godawfle Grittyfloor – Godric Gryffindor
Rotunda Radishgnaw – Rowena Ravenclaw
Spartan Silverfish – Salazar Slytherin
Snipe – Snape
Dorco Malfeasance – Draco Malfoy

— HORRIBLE HISTORY —

If Hogwarts had really existed in times gone by, it would have provided a valuable shelter for witches and wizards when they were getting a fatally bad press around Europe.

Down the centuries, those believed to be witches or wizards have inspired awe and fear in equal measure. They were people presumed to possess special powers that enabled them to change their shape or identity, become invisible, fly, cast spells, heal people, make them ill, curse them and kill them. In Greek and Roman times, witches were tolerated if they used their powers for good, although black witchcraft was punishable by law.

As Christianity spread, witchcraft became strongly associated with the Devil, and by the Middle Ages there was a vicious backlash – led by the Church – against those suspected of witchcraft. Inevitably, many ordinary people were swept up in the anti-witchcraft storm and died horrible deaths. Ironically, the name of the pope who urged his clergy to combat the 'heretical depravities' of witches in 1484 was Innocent VIII.

It was almost always women who were accused of using magic, and usually the old and/or unmarried ones, as the Church elders believed that women, being weak creatures, were more susceptible to the malevolent influences of the Devil. The evidence that accrued against these hapless women might range from the flimsy – like a poor harvest or a sick cow – to the downright absurd, including the ownership of a pet bird or cat or an unsightly birthmark. Females who weighed more than the Bible were also thought to be witches, as were those who were approached by beetles, mice or rats when they were held in dungeons. (As cells were infested with vermin, it was highly likely that the inmate would be compelled to keep the company of insects and rodents.)

Those accused of being witches often had to endure terrible torture and made up ludicrous stories simply to escape the agonies that would otherwise be inflicted upon them. Indeed, a large number died under torture before a confession could be wrung out of them. Of course, self-confessed witches were then burned at the stake (although some were strangled first) so that their bodies were purged of the Devil's effects by fire. JK Rowling's theory that real witches performed a flame-freezing charm and then pretended that they were in agony to satisfy the crowd may, sadly, be wide of the mark.

One estimate claims that as many as 200,000 people were executed for witchcraft within the space of 250 years. About half that number died in Germany alone, although all European countries were raked with witch fever. In England from 1644, Witchfinder General Matthew Hopkins made it

— HORRIBLE HISTORY (CONT'D) —

his holy mission to root out witches, using psychological torture to induce admissions by depriving the accused of sleep, food and company. About 400 people were sent to the gallows on Hopkins' say-so before public distaste drove him from office.

Even America suffered from witch hysteria after some children in the village of Salem were believed to be enchanted in 1692 after listening to scary stories told to them by the local minister's slave. Twenty died before the accusations and trials were halted. (See 'Witch Date 2' on pages 12–14.)

The last witch execution took place in Britain in 1684, while the final witch trial was held in 1712. In that case, Jane Wenham, known locally as a 'wise woman', was in the dock after a young servant girl threw a fit when she stood by her. Sixteen people gave evidence against Wenham, claiming among other things that she made magic ointment from dismembered corpses. Although she was sentenced to death, a far-sighted judge of the era campaigned for a reprieve and then a pardon. Later, it was found that the servant girl at the centre of the case was an epileptic, and it was this medical condition, rather than the presence of Jane Wenham, that caused convulsions. However, it wasn't until 1951 that witchcraft ceased to be a crime in Britain.

— WITCH DATE 4 —

The heads of Hogwarts, Beauxbatons and Durmstrang were injured during the Triwizard Tournament of 1792 when a cockatrice (another name for a basilisk) that the contestants were trying to capture went on the rampage. There is little evidence for such magical goings-on elsewhere, however, as the French Revolution was in full swing and guillotine use was on the rise. In the same year, the cornerstone of the White House – later to become one of America's most haunted venues – was laid. Perhaps most significantly of all, however, this year saw the patenting of the first flushing toilet, which later proved an ideal habitat for Moaning Myrtle and her kind.

— TWIN TALENTS —

There are at least two sets of twins at Hogwarts, and both sets are identical. This means that each set of twins came from the same ovarian egg, which split before the babies developed. Identical twins are always the same sex and, of course, look very similar. As they are so alike in appearance and temperament, George and Fred were both sorted into Gryffindor. However, Padma and Parvati – also identical twins – were sorted into different houses, Parvati joining Harry and company in Gryffindor while Padmil was destined for Ravenclaw.

There is, however, another type twin, known as *fraternal*, which means that the babies come from two different ovarian eggs. Fraternal twins can be different sexes, and frequently their appearances contrast radically from one another.

Not so long ago, twins were something of a rarity and two sets in a school would have been cause for comment. Now, though, there are more twins being born than ever before, although the rise corresponds only to the number of fraternal twins rather than identical twins. In Britain, about 15 in every 1,000 births result in twins, triplets or more, an increase of 20 per cent in 10 years – and that's only half the rate that America enjoys. In 2000, there were 118,916 twin births in the States as well as 6,742 triplet births, 506 sets of quadruplets and even 77 quintuplets. This adds up to a 74 per cent increase in the number of twin births in America since 1980. For American women, the chances of having a multiple birth stand at about three per cent.

There's a host of explanations for this. More women are resorting to fertility treatments, which might increase their chances of having twins. Also, many women delay having families until their 30s, which is when the frequency of multiple births inevitably rises.

Other well-known twins include tennis players Tim and Tom Gullikson, Australian cricketers Mark and Steve Waugh, soccer stars Frank and Ronald de Boer, Mary-Kate and Ashley Olson and Roz and Marilyn Borden (the *I Love Lucy* twins). Actor Vin Diesel has a twin brother, Paul, while Elvis and Liberace both had twins who died at birth.

— DRACO DORMIENS NUNQUAM TITILLANDUS —

At Hogwarts, the pupils are well versed in Latin, among other subjects. The names of spells are frequently in this obscure classical language, once used across almost the entire civilised world. Most of the spells do just what they say in Latin – for example, the name of the Lumos spell is taken from the Latin for 'light', while Expelliarmus is taken from the Latin for 'I drive out' (ie 'expel') and 'weapon'. According to Professor Dumbledore, one of the most useful Latin phrases known to wizards is the Hogwarts motto, 'Draco dormiens nunquam titillandus', which translates from Latin as 'Never tickle a sleeping dragon.'

This is undeniably an excellent selection of Latin words to use in the course of English exams or during conversation with your know-it-all uncle, but we Muggles might require other, less magical phrases for every day use. Here's a swift guide to some key expressions you can use to dazzle your teachers, friends and colleagues:

Ad infinitum – Endlessly
Ad nauseam – To the point where it makes one sick
Alma mater – The college or university to which one once belonged
Alter ego – Another or second self
Amor nummi – Love of money
Annus horribilis – Horrid year
Auribus teneo lupum – I am holding a wolf by the ears
Bona fides – In good faith; without malicious intent
Circa – On or about
Curriculum vitae – Career summary
De facto – In reality
Ergo – Therefore
Et cetera – And so forth
Finis – The end
In loco parentis – In place of a parent
Insanus omnis furere credit ceteros – All madmen think that everyone else is mad
In vitro – In a glass (commonly, a test tube)
Mea culpa – My fault
Non sequitur – It does not follow (ie the conclusion doesn't suit the argument)

Pax – Peace or truce
Persona non grata – Unacceptable person
Prima facie – At first sight
Qui docet discit – He who teaches also learns
Quid sit futurym cras fuge quaerere – Don't ask
    what's happening tomorrow
Quid pro quo – Fair exchange
Sic – Used to highlight an intentional mistake in
    original copy or a flag for an unintentional
    mistake in a quote
Status quo – Existing state of things
Tempus fugit – Time flies
Veni, vidi, vici – I came, I saw, I conquered
Via lactia – Milky Way
Victor ludorum – Sports champion

— CLASS ACTS —

When a British film magazine conducted a poll to discover
the identity of the greatest living movie stars over the age
of 50, two Harry Potter people came in the Top 30. The
survey, by *Empire* magazine, was topped by Robert de
Niro, but Alan Rickman – who has accrued a huge number
of new young fans with his role as Severus Snape – came
in at Number 19 while John Hurt (Mr Ollivander) was
Number 30.

— MEASURE OF SUCCESS —

Times have changed for JK Rowling, who began
writing for pleasure and has ended up at the head
of an international phenomenon. Still, all her
ambitions lie within the confines of the Harry Potter
series. She told one interviewer, 'If I can honestly
say to myself that, at the end of book seven, I wrote
the story that I set out to write and didn't change
one tiny thing because some reviewer had said,
"Let's have more feisty female footballers," if I can
look myself in the mirror and say I did it the way
I wanted, then I'm okay with it.'

— CHECK OUT CHESS HISTORY —

Hogwarts pupils play a particularly challenging form of chess, designed especially for wizards, where the pieces appear to have a will – or, at least, propulsion – of their own. Of the main characters, Ron is the most talented player of this game.

Of course, you don't have to be a budding witch or wizard to enjoy a game of chess. It's one of the world's oldest games, believed to have been conceived in either China or India centuries ago. When the Moors invaded Persia in about the eighth century, they discovered the locals playing the game and were soon hooked themselves. After that, wherever the Moors went, they took chess with them, which is how it came to southern Europe. Likewise, the well-travelled Vikings – frequent visitors to Moorish lands – helped to spread the popularity of chess to northern areas.

Without understanding much about Eastern history or the language originally attached to chess, the European players decided to frame it in terms they knew well. This is why the game features knights, castles and bishops, as the Church loomed large on the medieval landscape. Key pieces in the game are the king and queen, who, of

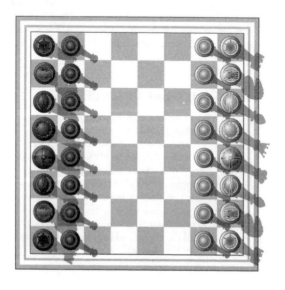

course, held ultimate power in feudal Europe, but spare a thought for the poor old pawns, representing the peasants or serfs. As it was in the game, so it was in life: they could never move far from their masters, they were easily expendable and they died early on in any conflict.

Years ago, chess pieces took the form of unique items of artwork, but in 1835 a simple design was created by chess fan Howard Staunton that was later adopted and endorsed by the chess-playing fraternity. This type of chess piece – probably the same as the set with which you play the game at home, with the king ranking the tallest – was named for Staunton and is the only type permitted in international chess competitions today.

— PARENTS ARE IMPORTANT —

Many children thrive under the tender loving care and guidance given freely by their parents, but not every child is fortunate enough to be with their mums and dads. JK Rowling was for many years a single parent and has had a bird's-eye view of the psychological hardships of a childhood spent without a father. No surprise, then, that there's oodles of empathy between her and hero Harry, who, after being orphaned, spent his young years in particularly nasty circumstances at the home of the Dursleys. And despite his occasional tantrums and bouts of self-obsession, Harry turned out to be basically a sound bloke.

Curiously, though, Voldemort also had parenting issues that were, in their way, equally traumatic. He began displaying worrying traits in childhood before becoming full-blown diabolical. By giving us an overview of his route to evil, Rowling illustrates that he wasn't necessarily born bad. So how is it that one parentless youngster is something of a model in morals while another is a fearsomely hopeless cause? The answer emerges via Dumbledore, who at various times points out to Harry that it is our choices that mark who we are, and also that Harry's ability to love makes him great while Voldemort's inability to feel that emotion dooms him to the dark side.

— I AIN'T AFRAID OF NO GHOST —

Harry and his pals are constantly running into the ghosts that haunt the Hogwarts corridors, enjoying their jokes and even their hospitality. However, although many people claim to have seen them, hard evidence supporting the existence of ghosts in Muggle territory is hard to come by. Dedicated ghost-hunters have been trying to nail the proof positive for years, and for anyone with a fascination for phantoms it's tempting to go out there and join them, but be warned: ghostbusting is an expensive business. Here's a list of the equipment you'd need to acquire before any self-respecting supernatural detective would take your ghost stories seriously.

CAMERA
You'll need one of these to snap the spectre when it appears – and not just any old camera will do. It's best to use one with 35mm film in black and white or infra-red, made especially for night photography. Every film has a different speed, and either 400 or 800 speeds are best for the purpose. You'll need to factor in film-development costs, too.

TRIPOD
Don't forget to take a tripod for the camera, because you're likely to get an attack of the shakes if an apparition appears.

VIDEO OR CAMCORDER
Movie footage of the phantom is much more persuasive evidence than photos.

TAPE RECORDER
A tape recorder with an external microphone should be in use throughout the ghost hunt in case there's a Moaning Myrtle-style ghost in the vicinity. The digital ones are best.

TORCHES
Take at least two, and don't forget to bring spare batteries.

ELECTROMAGNETIC FIELD DETECTOR
Ghosts have a habit of disrupting electromagnetic fields, so one of these gizmos should give a valuable clue when a spectre approaches. One cheap alternative is an old fashioned compass: watch for random needle-spinning as an indicator of a ghostly presence.

THERMOMETER
Everyone knows that the temperature drops suddenly when a ghost comes to call, and a thermometer will help you to chart any such thermal changes.

NOTEBOOK AND PEN
The cheapest of the necessary tools. Use them to make accurate, appropriate notes about what you see and hear. (Exaggerations and lies are easy to spot.) You might need to use the book as a sketchpad, too.

WRISTWATCH
Noting down when everything you see and hear occurs, and for how long, is an important part of record-keeping.

NIGHT-VISION EQUIPMENT
This is the nuts when it comes to helping you see in the dark. However, kitting out yourself, your camera and/or your camcorder with this type of gear is outrageously expensive. True, the costs are tumbling right now, but they're unlikely ever to fall to the level of pocket-money prices.

INFRARED THERMAL SCANNER
Such a device will pinpoint cold spots, even in cold weather, which will give you an idea where to train your camera lens.

MOBILE PHONE
Sometimes it's good to talk.

TAPE MEASURE
This will enable you to include distance measurements in your log entries.

DOWSING RODS
Usually used to track down water sources, L-shaped dowsing rods made of wood or metal are likely to sway towards an energy field.

Remember: never go on a ghost hunt without first seeking the advice of a professional.

— SPEAK EASY, JIM —

If you buy a Harry Potter audio book in the US, the voice you'll hear belongs to Jim Dale, a comedian who became a star of the British cinema and the American stage. Here are some facts about the man behind the voice:

- He was awarded an MBE (Member of the British Empire) in the Queen's Birthday Honours list in 2003.

- His most recent achievement is being a Guinness world record holder for recording the most character voices in an audio book.

- For three years he was a pop singer and was managed by George Martin, who also managed The Beatles.

- He is a veteran of 15 Carry On films, a series of slapstick comedy movies made in Britain from the 1960s.

- Throughout his career, he has preferred to perform his own stunts.

- He was one of the first people in America to read *Harry Potter And The Goblet Of Fire*, glimpsing the manuscript a month before the general publication date. (He had to sign a secrecy agreement with publishers before he was allowed to see the script.)

- He won a Tony Award and the Drama Desk Award for his portrayal of legendary circus ringmaster PT Barnum in the hit Broadway musical *Barnum*.

- His film credits also include the early-'80s Disney charmer *Pete's Dragon*.

- At the age of 17 he became the youngest professional comedian touring the variety music halls in Britain.

- He was once a disc jockey on BBC Radio.

- It took ten days for him to record the reading of *Harry Potter And The Goblet Of Fire*, at a rate of about 20 pages every hour.

- He won his first Grammy Award in 2000 for his interpretation of *Harry Potter And The Goblet Of Fire*.

- He wrote the lyrics to the hit song and film theme 'Georgie Girl' and won an Academy Award nomination for them.

INSPIRATIONS

With every new book, the pressure is on Jim to find new and distinctive voices for additional characters. On his website he has shared the inspiration behind some of his voice-overs, as follows:

- **Dobby** – Jim took this voice from that of a short actor who played Dopey in a musical of *Snow White And The Seven Dwarfs*. Dale met him in a lift when the vertically challenged fellow piped up, 'Excuse me, sir, you're wiping my nose with your bum.'

- **Professor McGonagall** – For this character, Jim replicates the voice of his Scottish aunt, who, like JK Rowling, lives in Edinburgh.

- **Professor Snape** – Here, Dale is mimicking the voice of a teacher he once had. 'He was so rotten to us, we pinned a large piece of raw fish under his office table-top,' Jim recalls. 'After two weeks of summer heat, even the school cat wouldn't go into the room.'

- **Hermione** – With this voice comes memories of his first girlfriend, who apparently spoke very quickly, saying she would never forgive herself if she left any words behind!

- **Moaning Myrtle** – He heard this ghost's voice from an unhappy girl telling her mother that her brother had swallowed her goldfish.

— FRY UP —

The man behind the voice on the Harry Potter audio books in the UK, meanwhile, is actor, director and writer Stephen Fry. He's probably best known for his appearances in comedies like the various Blackadder comedy series and *Jeeves And Wooster*, but there's a lot more to Stephen Fry than meets the eye!

STEPHEN FRY...
- Flies his own classic biplane
- Is a keen collector of teddy bears
- Once claimed the British record for saying the F-word on television the most times during a single live broadcast
- Loves cricket
- Is keen on Sherlock Holmes, the fictional detective created by Sir Arthur Conan Doyle
- Is a massive fan of poet and wit Oscar Wilde
- Went to jail for three months for credit-card fraud

— FRY UP (CONT'D) —

- Met Emma Thompson and sometime comic partner Hugh Laurie at Cambridge University
- Raises cash for the Terence Higgins Trust, an AIDS charity
- Stands over 6ft 4in tall
- Writes novels

FRY'S WISE WORDS

'I wish I were called Lemony Snicket.'

'An original idea. That can't be too hard. The library must be full of them.'

'I don't watch television. I think it destroys the art of talking about oneself.'

'The email of the species is more deadly than the mail.'

'When you've seen a nude infant doing a backwards somersault, you know why clothing exists.'

'It only takes a room of Americans for the English and Australians to realise how much we have in common.'

'I think animal testing is a terrible idea; they get all nervous and give the wrong answers.'

'Christmas to a child is the first terrible proof that to travel hopefully is better than to arrive.'

'Nudity is a deep worry if you have a body like a bin bag full of yoghurt, which I have.'

'A cousin of mine who was a casualty surgeon in Manhattan tells me that he and his colleagues had a one-word nickname for bikers: donors. Rather chilling.'

— MOVING ON —

Steve Kloves, the man who adapted the first four Harry Potter books for cinema, has stepped down from the demanding role. Instead, Kloves is going to rewrite another literary sensation for the camera, Mark Haddon's *The Curious Incident Of The Dog In The Night-time*. His role with Warner Bros is being taken by writer Michael Goldenberg, who will modify the epic *Harry Potter And The Order Of The Phoenix* for filming.

— WALKING TALL —

As a half-giant, Hagrid is tremendously tall – about twice the size of everyone else he walked alongside in London after first meeting Harry in *Harry Potter And The Philosopher's Stone*. If the average height of the British male is 5ft 10.5in (1.79m), that makes him in the region of 11ft 9in (3.58m) tall.

Nevertheless, there has been a human that would have been at Hagrid's shoulder, rather than at waist height. The world's tallest ever fella was Robert Wadlow (1918–40), from the US, who achieved a mighty 8ft 11in (2m 67.5cm) in height. Although in babyhood he appeared perfectly normal, size-wise, it is thought that an over-active pituitary gland brought on a growth spurt of outrageous proportions. Soon Wadlow towered over everyone around. His hands alone measured 12.75in (32.3cm) from wrist to middle fingertip. He became a shoe company's salesman, leaving his own boat-style footwear in his wake for stores to use in promotions. Ultimately, he died from an infected foot blister. It took a dozen men to carry his coffin to its final resting place. At his home town of Alton, Illinois, there's an inch-perfect statue of him to remind visitors of his lofty status.

Currently, the height accolade goes to Ukrainian Leonid Stadnik, who stands at 8ft 5in (2m 55cm) and is still growing. His excessive stature is making his life a misery, however, and if he gets much taller he faces having to enter his home on all fours. He trained as a vet but had to give up as cows and other animals were terrified of him. He can't fit into a motor vehicle, he needs specially made shoes and his fingers are too big to use a mobile telephone. Although he is accepted in his home village, he finds that he's a spectacle elsewhere. 'They brought me to the zoo and I felt myself an exhibit,' he once lamented. He believes a mistake in brain surgery that he underwent during his teenage years caused the abnormal inches to accrue.

— MERCHANDISE GUIDE —

On the back of every global phenomenon like Harry Potter comes a selection of themed toys and games costing anything from a few coins to a mighty wad of Muggle notes. Here's a brief survey of what's out there, star-rated in terms of desirability for the average Harry Potter fan.

Key: *   Steer well clear
       **   Think twice before buying
       ***   It won't change your life but you might want to give it a try
       ****   Find house room for this as soon as possible
       *****   Must have!

CHARACTER ART PORTFOLIO
Nine pictures of eminent Harry Potter characters on durable paper embellished with house crests, contained in an A3 wallet. A limited edition of 2,000.

** *(Unlikely to become a collectors' item. A series of posters would be a cheaper option.)*

LIMITED-EDITION COLLECTORS' PLATES
Various artwork decorates these fine china plates, issued in limited editions.

* *(These plates have a high risk of smashing as items fly bludger-style around your bedroom. Unless you want to eat your dinner off of one, what's the point?)*

HARRY POTTER LEGO HAGRID'S HUT
Depicting Hagrid and Hermione comforting one another after the loss of Buckbeak, this is one of many Lego kits available in the Harry Potter theme.

**** *(You never get too old for Lego.)*

REPLICA WAND
A wizard wand that looks like the one used by Harry in *Harry Potter And The Prisoner Of Azkaban*, measuring 35cm (14in).

* *(The makers call it 'an authentic recreation'. What's that all about?)*

MULTIMEDIA KEYBOARD
Although the keys look normal, the rest of the keyboard (that's the bit around the edge) is decorated with pictures of the Harry Potter cast.

** *(If you need a new keyboard, you might as well get this one. It won't make you a computer wizard, though, as that is an essentially Muggle skill.)*

DOUBLE-BUCKLE LEATHER BRIEFCASE
Smart satchel bearing Hogwarts school logo.

* *(No one should spend this kind of cash on a school bag.)*

HARRY POTTER SCARF
Made from 100 per cent wool, this is a cosy neck piece for a cold day and is distinguished by the Harry Potter mark.

*** *(If the price is too great then consider knitting your own.)*

HARRY POTTER LEVITATING PEN
A plastic ballpoint pen than appears to hold itself in mid-air above its holder.

* *(This 'technology' is nothing new, and there are many cheaper writing implements on the market.)*

HORNBY HARRY POTTER TRAIN SET, 2004
Electric toy train in the *Hogwarts Express* mould.

**** *(It's pricey, but what a joy it is to watch it in motion. Cheaper accessories are also available.)*

— OH, OH POTTER —

No one expects actor Daniel Radcliffe to play a schoolboy magician forever, and indeed fellow thespian Pierce Brosnan has already picked him out for a future role: that of super-suave spy James Bond. Brosnan has spent a decade as 007 and featured in four blockbuster Bond films. When it became clear he wasn't being considered for the role a fifth time, he said, 'For the next Bond, Colin Farrell would be great. But if you want to go even younger, Daniel Radcliffe. Give him a few years. You can see it, can't you? He'll be great. From Harry Potter to Bond.'

— THE OWL INFO SERVICE —

To Harry Potter and the rest of the pupils at Hogwarts, owls are majestic creatures that play a significant role in their daily lives. In Diagon Alley, Eeylops' Owl Emporium sells tawny, screech, barn, brown and snowy owls to prospective pupils. However, the rest of us Muggles are hardly ever aware of owls and only ever see them if they are caged in zoos. Here are some facts you should know about owls:

1. There are 216 species of owl, separated into two families. The smallest is the elf owl, which is the size of a sparrow, while the largest, with a wingspan of 6ft (2m), is the Eurasian eagle owl.

2. The name of a group of owls together is a 'parliament'.

3. Snowy owls, like the one given to Harry by Hagrid, have yellow eyes.

4. All owls have eyes that face forwards, rather than having them set at each side of their head, like other birds. This helps them judge depth when they're hunting.

5. When they turn their heads, owls can cover 270 degrees. That's three-quarters of a full circle.

6. A barn owl is said to be able to hear the heartbeat of a mouse in the same 30ft² (9m²) room.

7. According to a 15-year-long survey carried out by the Barn Owl Trust in the UK, half of all known barn-owl deaths occur on roads.

8. Tawny owls talk to each other. When one bird makes the familiar 'too-wit' sound, another will reply 'too-whoo'.

9. Barn owls have one ear slightly higher than the other to make their hearing that much more acute.

10. In flight, an owl is noiseless.

11. Snowy owls are largely silent. (Hedwig, of course, is the exception to this rule.)

12. Owls wink by bringing their eyelids down, much as we do, while other birds lift the bottom flap of skin upwards to meet the top lash.

— FOREVER BLOWING BUBBLES —

Quidditch is the game that's on the lips of every self-respecting Hogwarts pupil, but there is one who confesses to liking that other beautiful game: football. Dean Thomas, a pupil who shares Harry and Ron's dormitory, is a West Ham fan. (At one point in the Harry Potter saga, Ron tries to make the players in Dean's team poster move by prodding them into action, something many fans and managers have yearned to do on numerous occasions over the years.) JK Rowling freely admits that she makes mention of the east London team to please a long-time pal who is a fanatical fan. (The same friend is identified as Troy in the Irish Quidditch team.) If you're a committed Harry Potter fan, you probably know more about Quidditch than you do about footie, so here are some West Ham facts to help balance things out.

- West Ham has a longstanding history, having been formed in 1895 as Thames Ironworks FC, whose players came from the local shipbuilding foundry. The name change happened five years later, although the team's nickname, 'the Hammers', maintains a link with the club's industrial past.

- The team has played at Upton Park (correctly known as the Boleyn Ground, Upton Park) since 1904. One curious fact about the Hammers is that they have had just ten managers in a history of 110 years, fewer than any

— FOREVER BLOWING BUBBLES (CONT'D) —

other senior club, with the exception of Boston United and Rushden and Diamonds, while those clubs have been in existence for a shorter spell.

• The club theme tune is 'I'm Forever Blowing Bubbles', which has echoed around the ground on a bi-weekly basis since the 1920s.

• Perhaps the most famous West Ham players ever to grace a pitch were Bobby Moore, Geoff Hurst and Martin Peters, who as captain and goal scorers were all significant members of the 1966 England World Cup-winning squad. However, the team has had a selection of acclaimed players who have names that wouldn't look out of place in any Harry Potter novel, such as Billy Bonds, Syd Puddefoot, Jimmy Ruffell and Ronnie Boyce.

— ERROR TERROR —

When JK Rowling was sat in a café, writing exciting instalments of the first Harry Potter adventure, she could hardly have imagined what lay in store: fame, fortune and literary recognition. Nor was she aware how people would pore over her every word, devising hidden meanings and analysing dreams and themes, and indeed she might have carried out just one more manuscript inspection had she but known the minute inspection to which her words would be subjected. All authors make mistakes, so JK should be cut a bit a slack for not always tying up literary loose ends as neatly as she might have done. Even so, we couldn't resist including some errors spotted in her books. There might even be creative explanations that mitigate in their favour. See what you think.

• Enraged by the Dursleys' non-cooperation and child cruelty in Chapter 4 of *Harry Potter And The Philosopher's Stone*, Hagrid uses magic to give Dudley a pig's tail. Presumably, the island on which they find themselves is very much in the Muggle world, as it is Vernon Dursley who locates it, yet there are no consequences for Hagrid, even though use of magic in Muggle territory usually ends in serious strife for the transgressing wizard, as dictated by the existing Improper Use of Magic legislation. As Harry remains with Hagrid, he would have noticed if action had been taken against Hagrid by the Ministry, who are aware of illegal magic being carried out without needing to be told. Nor do we know how Dudley dealt with the spell, or indeed whether or not he has the piggy tail to this day.

• Also in *Harry Potter And The Philosopher's Stone*, Tom, the old bar tender in the Leaky Cauldron, greets Harry with the words 'Welcome back, Mr

Potter, welcome back.' Are we to assume that licensing laws in the wizard world are so lax that the infant Harry Potter would have been a regular there?

- Slytherin is known for its preference for pure-bloods. Curiously, Voldemort – himself once a Slytherin – is a half-blood, as he confessed to Harry in *Harry Potter And The Goblet Of Fire*, in which he says that his father was 'a Muggle and a fool'. Nor is he the only one.

- Dobby and other house elves can apparate around Hogwarts when, as Hermione continually reminds us, there are charms in force to stop the practice happening.

- In a similar vein, Harry uses both a watch and an alarm clock at Hogwarts when we've been told that Muggle technology doesn't work there.

- In *Harry Potter And The Goblet Of Fire*, Harry learns from the pensieve that Augustus Rookwood, an officer at the Department of Mysteries, is named by Karkaroff as a Voldemort spy. However, in *Harry Potter And The Order Of The Phoenix*, mention of Rookwood in *The Daily Prophet* gives his name as Algernon. Presumably, it's a case of not believing what's in the newspapers?

- The boa constrictor at London Zoo winks at Harry – which is stranger than you might think, because snakes have immoveable eyelids. (That's the way you can tell the difference between a snake and a reptile, the latter of which does have the ability to wink.)

- Dennis Creevey comes with brother Colin to the Hog's Head in Hogsmeade for the first DA meeting, which is curious because Hogwarts pupils aren't permitted into the village until they're in their third year. At this time, Dennis was only in his second year, having joined in *Harry Potter And The Goblet Of Fire*.

- In *Harry Potter And The Order Of The Phoenix*, Harry and Hermione watch the final match of the Quidditch season, having 'found seats in the topmost row of the stands'. When Hagrid arrives, he had apparently 'squeezed his way along the row behind'. Evidently an additional row appeared after Harry and Hermione took their seats.

- In *Harry Potter And The Philosopher's Stone*, a woman is overheard in Diagon Alley complaining about the price of dragon liver, at 17 sickles an ounce. That's odd phrasing, because 17 sickles equals a galleon.

— WITCH DATE 5 —

In *Harry Potter And The Order Of The Phoenix*, Harry is charged with having committed an offence against the Decree for the Reasonable Restriction of Underage Sorcery, 1875. This was a significant year for Muggles interested in the dark arts, too, for it was when the Theosophical Society – a sort of spiritual talking shop – was formed and Aleister Crowley, a notorious occultist who allegedly advised Churchill on how to counter Hitler's hexes, was born.

— MUSIC MAN —

Arguably the biggest star to figure in the first three Harry Potter movies never appears on the screen. John Williams, who wrote the soundtrack to the first three Harry Potter films to great acclaim, is a phenomenally successful composer who has notched up more stunning film themes than many people have had cinema trips.

But that's not all. Williams is also behind numerous TV tunes that you've hummed to yourself while you've been doing the washing up. On top of that, he has penned symphonies and the scores for several Olympic Games opening ceremonies. He's equally at home with opera, orchestras, jazz and pop.

Williams was born in Long Island, New York, in 1932, and his father was a percussionist of some renown. As a teenager, John dreamed of becoming a concert pianist and premiered his first original piece, a piano sonata, at the age of 19. After studying music at university he worked in TV on theme tunes for series including *Lost In Space*, *Gilligan's Island* and *Voyage To The Bottom Of The Sea*, all of which turned out to be mega-hits of the era. Later, transferring his skills to Hollywood, with considerable panache he knocked out big-sound theme tunes, each with a distinctive quality. Blockbuster director Steven Spielberg became a particular fan. By 2002, Williams had earned an amazing 42 Oscar nominations and secured five of them. He also has 17 Grammys, three Golden Globes, two Emmys and five BAFTA Awards under his belt. If you're still not sure whether or not you know any of his music, here's a list of just 20 of the themes for films or series of films identified with him.

Jurassic Park
Indiana Jones
Star Wars
Catch Me If You Can
ET: The Extraterrestrial
AI: Artificial Intelligence
Pearl Harbor
Jaws
Angela's Ashes
Rugrats: The Movie
Saving Private Ryan
Home Alone
Superman
The Big Chill
Airplane!
Earthquake
The Towering Inferno
The Poseidon Adventure
Minority Report
Schindler's List

— WHAT'S IN A NAME? 2 —

She's Jo to her friends and Joanne Kathleen to the serried ranks of British bureaucracy, but to her legions of fans she remains JK Rowling. That's because her publisher, Bloomsbury, believed boys would not buy a book about a youthful wizard and his adventures if they believed it was written by a woman. So her Christian name was vetoed in order to help disguise her full identity.

— POTTED POTTER —

If you haven't yet read Harry Potter I–V and you want to know what's happened so far, here's a potted history. There's much more to each plot that is described here, along with a host of fascinating characters, so a brief guide can't replace the original text. Nevertheless, here are some bare-bones versions of the first five books for those too daunted to tackle the ever-increasing volumes or who read the books so long ago they've forgotten the story. (If you're ever stuck for a party game among fellow Potter fans, why not try to summarise the plot of each tome in as few words as you can?)

HARRY POTTER AND THE PHILOSOPHER'S STONE

Orphan Harry Potter lives in the cupboard under the stairs in the house of his aunt and uncle, Vernon and Petunia Dursley, until he receives a letter telling him that (a) he's a wizard and (b) he is to start at Hogwarts School of Witchcraft and Wizardry. Soon he learns that his parents were killed by evil wizard Lord Voldemort, not in a car crash as he believed. As a baby, it turns out, Harry was also attacked by Voldemort, but his mother's love protected him, although he was forever marked by a lightning-shaped scar on his forehead.

Harry catches the *Hogwarts Express* from platform 9¾ at King's Cross Station in London, joins Gryffindor – one of four houses at the school – and learns to play Quidditch, a broomstick-based sport, at which he excels. He finds firm friends in Ron Weasley and Hermione Granger, but he becomes enemies with fellow pupil Draco Malfoy and teacher Severus Snape. The action begins when Harry discovers the existence of the magical and mysterious Philosopher's Stone (originally held to be an elixir of life), which he must secure before Lord Voldemort in order to stop the latter's return to power.

HARRY POTTER AND THE CHAMBER OF SECRETS

Harry's life is grim back at the Dursleys' and is made worse by the arrival of Dobby, a house elf owned by the Malfoys. However, Harry is liberated by the Weasley family in a flying Ford Anglia that eventually takes him and Ron back to Hogwarts.

Problems begin for Harry when fellow pupils start turning into stone and he is blamed. Hermione is put out of action, Hagrid is wrongfully arrested and a mysterious diary has everyone perplexed. Eventually, Harry gains access to the Chamber of Secrets with an urgent mission to complete.

HARRY POTTER AND THE PRISONER OF AZKABAN

Convicted murderer Sirius Black escapes from the wizard prison Azkaban and seems to have his sights set on Harry Potter. After illegally performing magic against an odious relative, Harry escapes the Dursleys and catches the Knight Bus to London before going to Hogwarts.

On the train, Harry meets the spooky Azkaban guards known as Dementors and is overcome. Back at Hogwarts, he concentrates on Quidditch, despite being unsettled by a prediction of his death issued in his Divination class. Draco Malfoy is hurt in another class while Harry crashes out of a Quidditch match and Hermione is caught up with her busy timetable. Later, Harry discovers that the felon Sirius, who apparently betrayed his parents, is his godfather.

Harry seeks help in protecting himself from the Dementors while Ron and Hermione fall out over their respective pets, Scabbers the rat and Crookshanks the cat, and Hagrid has problems with his pet, Buckbeak the Hippogriff. When Sirius Black sneaks into Hogwarts, everyone is on their guard, although it doesn't affect the outcome of the

— POTTED POTTER (CONT'D) —

Quidditch Cup. Harry discovers some extraordinary revelations after Ron is dragged from the school grounds by a giant black dog.

HARRY POTTER AND THE GOBLET OF FIRE

Harry attends the Quidditch World Cup finals with the Weasleys, but the occasion is marred by the appearance in the sky of the dark mark: Voldemort's calling card. At Hogwarts, pupils learn that the year ahead will be fashioned by the resumption of the Triwizard Tournament, involving two other wizarding schools in addition to Hogwarts. Unusually, Harry is chosen to participate.

Ron falls out with Harry, who must seek alternative help in unravelling the clues laid before him for the Triwizard Tournament. Ultimately, Harry is captured and must witness Voldemort's return to full magical health.

HARRY POTTER AND THE ORDER OF THE PHOENIX

Grumpy with adolescent anxieties as well as the small matter of having an evil wizard on his case, Harry is in an explosive mood when he finally meets up with Ron and Hermione. He's also hauled before a Ministry of Magic tribunal before returning to school. When he arrives at Hogwarts, the Sorting Hat warns of treacherous times at the school, and the arrival of a new teacher seems to bear out its words.

Harry leads a newly formed group that practises Defence against the Dark Arts, despite the Ministry's insistence that Voldemort is not a threat. He feels uncomfortable after getting a surprising insight into his father and is even more disturbed by a series of dreams.

Meanwhile, school life isn't half as much fun as it

used to be, not least because Harry, Ron and Hermione must take important exams. As the acute pressure of school life reaches its peak, Harry and friends encounter Voldemort's faithful sidekicks in a tussle for ultimate power as the Dark Lord attempts to resolve longstanding questions over an old prophecy.

— TRUTH AND LIES —

- JK Rowling wrote *Harry Potter And The Philosopher's Stone* on café napkins because she couldn't afford paper. *(No. She used a notebook.)*

- She wrote in cafés because she was too poor to heat and light her flat. *(Wrong again. She found that baby Jessica slept better after being wheeled around in her pushchair. The author then capitalised on her free time.)*

- The account of platform 10 at King's Cross better describes another station, Euston. *(True. JK Rowling has admitted she was picturing Euston in her mind's eye when she wrote the text. As she was living in Manchester at the time, she could not check the accuracy of her description.)*

- JK Rowling drew a series of pictures to illustrate her manuscript. *(True. She's a talented artist as well as a writer.)*

- The man who agreed to publish *Harry Potter And The Philosopher's Stone* told JK Rowling not to give up her day job. *(True. Barry Cunningham at Bloomsbury told her there was no money to be earned in children's books.)*

- JK Rowling is richer than the Queen. *(True, according to* The Sunday Times' *Rich List, which puts Rowling, with a fortune of £280 million, some 11 places higher than the Queen, at 122nd place. However, JK has noticeably fewer castles to her name. The answer to this numerical anomaly appears to be that the Queen was hit by a slump in stocks and shares while Rowling's coffers benefited from better-than-ever sales of Potter merchandise.)*

— THE NUMBERS GAME —

4 Privet Drive is the house number and address of the Dursleys.

7 books will complete the Harry Potter series.

7 players in a Quidditch team.

7 is the number on Harry's Quidditch robes.

11 inches is the length of Harry's wand.

15 first chapters originally written for *Harry Potter And The Philosopher's Stone* were discarded.

17 sickles to a galleon.

27 weeks is the length of time Gilderoy Lockhart's autobiography *Magical Me* has spent in the best sellers list when Harry, Ron and Hermione go to Diagon Alley in *Harry Potter And The Chamber Of Secrets* to buy their books.

29 knuts to a sickle.

55 per cent of all Harry Potter books are sold in the USA.

68 is the age of Lord Voldemort when he returns to full power in *Harry Potter And The Goblet Of Fire*.

85th place is the spot that JK Rowling occupies in *Forbes* magazine's list of the world's most powerful women. She is one of only six British women to make the list.

170 is the score with which Ireland won the Quidditch World Cup.

390 is Sirius Black's prison number.

442nd Quidditch World Cup final was won by Ireland.

713 is the number of the vault from which Hagrid retrieves the Philosopher's Stone at Gringotts.

7 Horcruxes wrought by Voldemort.

17 chapters in *Harry Potter And The Philosopher's Stone*.

18 chapters in *Harry Potter And The Chamber Of Secrets*.

22 chapters in *Harry Potter And The Prisoner Of Azkaban*.

37 chapters in *Harry Potter And The Goblet Of Fire*.

38 chapters in *Harry Potter And The Order Of The Phoenix*.

30 chapters in *Harry Potter And The Half-Blood Prince*.

62 is the number of languages into which the Harry Potter books have been translated.

2,000 is the number of copies published in the first Harry Potter book's puny initial print run.

— GOING UNDERGROUND —

At first glance, it seems highly unlikely that Gringotts, the goblin bank, with its vaults guarded by dragons, could be in the bowels of London. (When Hagrid says it lies 'hundreds of miles under London', he's probably over-exaggerating because it gets pretty hot down there.) However, it's true that there is a lot more below the streets of London than you might at first think.

Down there lies hundreds of tunnels, chambers and catacombs – not to mention sewers – many of which are as yet uncharted, having been constructed in ages past. Indeed, in the 16th, 17th and 18th centuries, numerous people lived underground throughout the city in basement, cellar or tunnel dwellings, rarely seeing the light of day.

Had Harry travelled beneath London at such vast depths as Hagrid quotes, it's likely that he would have spotted fossils, because some dating back 50 million years were discovered during the construction of Victoria Underground Station.

What's even more amazing, though, is that, unlike today's modern metal tubes, the first underground trains operating beneath London were open carriages, just like the one that took Harry, Hagrid and Griphook to the bank safe. As the engine pulling the carriages on the trial trip of the London Underground between Paddington and

— GOING UNDERGROUND (CONT'D) —

Farringdon Road in 1863 was powered by steam and the rail engineering was comparatively primitive, it is likely that the travellers felt every bit as sick at the end of their trip as Harry was at the end of his.

Times have since changed, of course, and it's unlikely that the Gringotts cart could manage the speeds of modern Tube trains, whose average speed is 20.5mph (33kph), while the deepest station is Hampstead at 192ft (58.5m) beneath the street. Every year, each Tube train used on the Underground system travels the equivalent mileage of London to Sydney, Australia, seven times over. Indeed, the tube carries as many individual people each year as there are living Down Under.

Confusingly, most of the train system we know as the London Underground actually lies above ground. Indeed, there are many quirky things about the Underground that are too irresistible to leave out, even when they are not strictly relevant. For instance, according to www.going-underground.net, there is only one Tube station name out of all 287 that doesn't have any letters of the word 'mackerel' in it (St John's Wood), all 409 escalators do the equivalent of two round-the-world trips every week, and back when escalators were first invented, in 1911, not only were they made of wood but a man with wooden legs by the name of Bumper Harris was employed to travel up and down them to prove that they were safe. The spookiest places on the Underground, meanwhile, are the 40 or so disused or 'ghost' stations that are unlit and swiftly bypassed by today's trains. These include British Museum, South Kentish Town, York Road and King William Street.

— WINGED MESSENGERS —

At Hogwarts, the postal system is run by obliging owls who give a first-class service, arriving with letters and parcels grasped firmly in their talons. Yet, although owls do occasionally feature in public flying shows and in recent years have become trendy pets, there's no likelihood that in reality they would ever cut it as postal workers.

However, the notion of avian messengers is not a new one. In ancient times, one of the earliest methods of getting post across the miles was to use carrier pigeons, which bore the news to remote areas of far-flung empires. Additionally, they were also cooked up in culinary dishes (as an ingredient, they're known as 'squab'), and their prodigious production of poo provided a potent fertiliser.

No doubt those in classical cultures were, like us, also perplexed by the age-old pigeon question: why do you never see baby pigeons? The answer appears to be that pigeon nests are well hidden and that pigeon babies are spoiled rotten by their parents, never having to leave the security of the roost to search for food until they're fully fledged. Young pigeons are fed on a cheesy-looking milk regurgitated by their parents – although that might be a case of too much information. Suffice to say that they grow fat and glossy before they ever show themselves to their public. Alas, there's no answer to that other timeless poser: why do pigeons poo on your shoulder and not the person next to you?

Anyway, the humble carrier pigeon continued stacking up its illustrious achievements in more recent times. The first Reuters news agency was actually a line of pigeon posts, while as many as 300,000 pigeons flew for the Allies during the two world wars and were especially useful for ferrying information about undercover operations. Indeed, pigeons were such effective runners (*sic*) that, at French coastal ports during the Second World War, the occupying Germans kept a ready supply of hawks that would prey upon the returning postbirds. Indeed, one Exeter-based pigeon made it home after her neck and breast had been torn open by a hawk. After two months of recuperation, she was back in action – only to be shot in the wing and body.

Strictly speaking, the bird we know as a homing pigeon is, in fact, a variety of dove. Today's racing pigeons – distinguishable from their domestic cousins by a band around one or both legs – have been developed by breeding together several different pigeon varieties.

Bizarrely, a ten-year scientific study into how homing pigeons get home came up with an astonishing theory: they follow motorways and trunk roads, just like we do. To conduct this study, researchers at Oxford University used the latest satellite tracking devices in their bid to unravel one of the mysteries of nature. True, the birds use their fabulous internal navigational system for a first-time trip, but on consequent flights it's easier for them to use the existing road network as a reference. Professor Tim Guilford reveals, 'It's striking to see the pigeons fly straight down the A434 Oxford bypass and then sharply curve off at the traffic lights before curving off again at the roundabout.'

— MAGIC MENTORS —

Here are some snippets of wise, uplifting words of Hogwarts' Dumbledore and Middle-Earth's Gandalf. Are they...could they be...related?

DUMBLEDORE	GANDALF
To the well-organised mind, death is but the next great adventure.	You don't really suppose, do you, that all your adventures and escapes were managed by mere luck, just for your sole benefit?
Fear of a name increases fear of the thing itself.	What do you mean? Do you wish me a good morning, or mean that it is a good morning whether I want it or not, or that you feel good this morning or that it is a morning to be good on?
It was one of my more brilliant ideas and, between you and me, that's saying something.	If I say he is a burglar, a burglar he is, or will be when the time comes.
It does not do to dwell on dreams and forget to live.	This is not my adventure. I may look in on it again before it is all over, but in the meantime I have some other pressing business to attend to.
The truth. It is a beautiful and terrible thing, and should therefore be treated with great caution.	[Sauron] is seeking [the Ring], seeking it, and all his strength is bent on it. It is his great hope and our great fear.
It is our choices, Harry, that show what we truly are, far more than our abilities.	Take courage, Lord of the Mark, for better help you will not find. No counsel have I to give to those that despair.
I think all this merits a good feast.	Look out for me, especially at unlikely times.
Indifference and neglect often do more damage than outright dislike	Let us remember that a traitor may betray himself and do good that he does not intend.

DUMBLEDORE	GANDALF
Old men are guilty if they forget what it was to be young.	None of you have any weapon that could hurt me. Be merry! We meet again at the turn of the tide.
To have been loved so deeply…will give us some protection for ever.	All worthy things that are in peril as the world now stands, those are my care… For I also am a steward. Did you not know?

Of course, there are many more examples of parallels between the Harry Potter series and other children's books. Here's a selection of similar works:

TITLE: *The Lion, The Witch And The Wardrobe*, part of the Narnia series by CS Lewis

HERO/HEROINE: Lucy

IMPORTANT PALS: Edmund, Susan, Peter and Mr Otter

SAGE: Aslan

VILLAIN: The White Witch

WHERE DOES IT ALL UNFOLD? Narnia

BLUFFERS' GUIDE TO THE PLOT: Through the back of a wardrobe, the children reach Narnia, where it is always winter but never Christmas. They are told by an otter to save Aslan, who has been turned to stone by the White Witch

HANDY TO HAVE: A wardrobe with an unexpected exit

WHAT'S THE WORST THAT COULD HAPPEN? They could be turned to stone alongside Aslan and Narnia could be forgotten

THEME: Good versus evil

TITLE: His Dark Materials trilogy (comprising *Northern Lights*, *The Subtle Knife*, *The Amber Spyglass/The Golden Compass*) by Philip Pullman

HERO/HEROINE: Lyra Belagque, who is one determined young woman and gets emotionally involved

IMPORTANT PALS: Will Parry (user of the Subtle Knife), Iorek Byrnison (an armoured bear)

SAGE: n/a

VILLAINS: Mrs Coulter, some angels

WHERE DOES IT ALL UNFOLD? Oxford, numerous different dimensions

BLUFFERS' GUIDE TO THE PLOT: Lyra's best friend is kidnapped. She goes looking for him and meets up with Will. Together they go into alternative universes in order to save the world

HANDY TO HAVE: A daemon – ie a being attached to every person in Lyra's world. Hers is called Pantalaimon

— MAGIC MENTORS (CONT'D) —

WHAT'S THE WORST THAT COULD HAPPEN? In *Northern Lights*, it is the death of a friend. In *The Subtle Knife*, it's spectres on the rampage. Finally, it's the rise of the angels and the end of the world

THEME: Good versus evil

TITLE: *Artemis Fowl*, *The Arctic Incident* and *The Eternity Code* – various adventures by Eoin Colfer

HERO/HEROINE: Holly Short

IMPORTANT PALS: Butler (Artemis's bodyguard), Juliette (his sister)

SAGE: Foaly, a centaur, who is chief technical consultant – a real brains

VILLAIN: Artemis Fowl

WHERE DOES IT ALL UNFOLD? Either at Artemis's house or in a fairy world

BLUFFERS' GUIDE TO THE PLOT: Artemis wants to get rich, so he kidnaps Holly and holds her to ransom

HANDY TO HAVE: Butler, who puts his life on the line countless times for Artemis

WHAT'S THE WORST THAT COULD HAPPEN? Ordinary human folk could find out about fairies

THEME: Evil versus good

TITLE: *A Series Of Unfortunate Events: The Bad Beginning* by Lemony Snicket

HERO/HEROINE: Violet Baudelaire

IMPORTANT PALS: Violet's brother and sister, Klaus and Sunny

SAGE: Justice Strauss

VILLAIN: Count Olaf

WHERE DOES IT ALL UNFOLD? Places unknown

BLUFFERS' GUIDE TO THE PLOT: The relentlessly evil Count Olaf tries to get his hands on a fortune belonging to three orphaned children

HANDY TO HAVE: Books and the power of invention

WHAT'S THE WORST THAT COULD HAPPEN? The evil count marries Violet and kills off Sunny

THEME: Good versus evil

TITLE: *The Sword In The Stone* by TH White

HERO/HEROINE: Wart

IMPORTANT PALS: Sir Kay, sometimes

SAGE: Merlyn

VILLAIN: Morgana

WHERE DOES IT ALL UNFOLD? In Sir Ector's castle in ye olde England

BLUFFERS' GUIDE TO THE PLOT: Wart is tutored by Merlyn the wizard in preparation for kingship

HANDY TO HAVE: The sword, fresh from the stone (shades of Harry Potter here, as Harry pulls Godric's blade out of the Sorting Hat)

WHAT'S THE WORST THAT COULD HAPPEN? The sword stays stuck fast in the stone

THEME: Good versus evil

— WHIMSICAL THOUGHTS —

If the bookshelf featured on her website is anything to go by, JK Rowling is a fan of Dorothy L Sayers. A Rector's daughter, Dorothy Leigh Sayers went to Somerville College, Oxford, where she earned a first-class honours degree in Modern Languages. She was best known for her series of detective stories featuring hero Lord Peter Wimsey, although she also wrote plenty of plays, poetry and acclaimed literary translations as well. By the outbreak of the Second World War, she devoted hours debating theology, and she numbered CS Lewis (another Rowling favourite) among her friends. However, Sayers also made a parallel reputation for herself for writing witty, incisive remarks, many of which have been absorbed into common speech. Here's a selection of the best:

> *'Trouble shared is trouble halved.'*

> *'The great advantage about telling the truth is that nobody ever believes it.'*

> *'A human being must have occupation if he or she is not to become a nuisance to the world.'*

> *'As I grow older and older, and totter towards the tomb, I find that I care less and less who goes to bed with whom.'*

> *'She always says, my lord, that facts are like cows: if you look them in the face hard enough, they generally run away.'*

> *'The first thing a principle does is kill somebody.'*

> *'Time and trouble will tame an advanced young woman, but an advanced old woman is uncontrollable by any earthly force.'*

> *'Every time a man expects, as he says, his money to work for him, he is expecting other people to work for him.'*

— THE WORLD'S MOST HAUNTED HOUSES —

The selection of benign spooks gliding around the corridors of Hogwarts appear at first sight to be bizarre, but sharing a home with ghosts isn't as uncommon as you might think. There are plenty of candidates for the accolade of most haunted house (not least the Shrieking Shack), but here are a few Muggle candidates to whet your appetite.

The Whaley House in San Diego, California, was apparently built on land that was once a cemetery and has since been the focus of numerous ghostly encounters. Independent witnesses believe that the smell of cigar smoke or perfume often lingers in the air, from no apparent source, and the window shutters open and close at will. The restless spirits behind the unearthly events are believed to be those of a young girl accidentally hanged on the property, a thief clubbed to death by an angry crowd and a child of the house's original builder.

Raynham Hall in Norfolk is apparently haunted by 'the Brown lady', a noblewoman in a brown satin dress whose eyes are missing from their sockets. The hall came to prominence after the ghost was inadvertently photographed in 1936 as part of a feature for *Country Life* magazine, producing what is believed to be among the most apparently authentic ghost pics in existence.

The White House, home to the incumbent American president, is also notorious for housing the ghosts of past presidents and first ladies who clearly don't relish the prospect of returning to a more humble abode. Most eminent among the ghosts is that of President Abraham Lincoln, seen surveying the lawns from the Oval Office window, perched on a bed pulling off his boots and knocking on bedroom doors after dark. Lincoln (1809–65) was assassinated in the Ford Theater, Washington, just days after the end of the American Civil War.

Hampton Court is a riverside palace built by King Henry VIII, who – according to some accounts – still resides there. It is the ghostly presence of some of his six wives, however, that are most often reported. Jane Seymour, his third wife, who in 1537 died just one week after giving birth to the future King Edward VI, is associated with the Clock Tower. The screams of Catherine Howard, meanwhile, are occasionally heard from 'the Haunted Gallery' as she pleads for her life to a vengeful husband in 1542, after being convicted of treason. The young king's nurse, Mrs Sybil Penn, is also a spectral visitor, lately dubbed 'the lady in grey', while Cardinal Wolsey and architect Sir Christopher Wren, who designed an addition to the palace, are both thought to have made appearances there subsequent to their deaths.

Apparitions have also infested the Tower of London, a palace built by William the Conquer but that also acted as a jail and place of execution for many eminent Brits. Among them are the ghosts of King Edward V and his brother, Richard, Duke of York, both of whom were murdered in boyhood (probably in 1483) by an unknown assailant. The ghost of Anne Boleyn, Henry VIII's second wife and mother of Queen Elizabeth I, is also often seen there, sometimes with and sometimes without her head, after being executed by a swordsman in 1536 on charges of adultery and treason, while also included in the long list of ghostly personages to appear at the tower is King Henry VI and explorer Sir Walter Raleigh.

— THE THINGS THEY SAY ABOUT HARRY POTTER —

'I found myself struggling to finish a tedious, badly written version of Billy Bunter on broomsticks.'

– Anthony Holden

'Rowling's comic timing is brilliant, perfect. Her books are beautifully paced and are a mixture of school magic and beyond. They'll be bought by future generations of children, and adults too.'

– Times literary critic Nicolette Jones

'Harry Potter is saying you can dabble in witchcraft as long as it's entertaining. If it's not good, it's evil. There ain't no in-between.'

*– Beverley Green, Sunday-school teacher from
Eastman, Georgia, to Wired.com reporter
Julia Scheeres*

'I really wrote it entirely for myself. It is my sense of humour in the books, not what I think children will find funny, and I suppose that would explain some of the appeal to adults.'

– JK Rowling

'I didn't want there to be so many people here, because this is MY book.'
*– A 12-year-old girl who went to see JK Rowling read some
of her latest work at the Edinburgh Book Festival*

'Having read it, I was immersed completely in the Harry Potter world. I recognised that this was something exceptionally clever and very good and very well written, with a prospect of six more books to follow.'

– Jim Dale

'Scarcely higher than a Spice Girls lyric.'

– Anthony Holden

'I have read Harry Potter books. I have researched them thoroughly, and my personal opinion is that they are witchcraft manuals.'
*– Cheryllyn Dudley, MP for the African Christian
Democratic Party in South Africa*

'The world of magic is the world of imagination. Harry discovers he's on a journey to learn who he is, to learn the difference between good and evil. And in his world, Harry tries to overcome those challenges. It turns out that love

is what sustains Harry. That is faith. That is what faith is about, and the books are a journey of the imagination.'
– Rev Jeff Champlin, St Bartholomew's Episcopal Church, Arkansas, USA

'Personally, I've never understood the hype about Harry Potter. I've seen one of the films (I was stuck on a long-haul flight and didn't have much choice) and tried to read one of the books and was left distinctly unimpressed.'
– The BBC's Robert Winder

'I think JK Rowling has done more for literacy around the world than any single [other] human being.'
– Gordon Brown, Chancellor of the Exchequer

'[Harry Potter books] are subtle seductions that act unnoticed and, by this, deeply distort Christianity in the soul before it can grow properly.'
– Pope Benedict XVI

'[The world of Harry Potter] is written for people whose imaginative lives are confined to TV cartoons, and the exaggerated (more exciting, not threatening) mirror-worlds of soaps, reality TV and celebrity gossip.'
– Author AS Byatt

'JK Rowling's work should come with an intellectual health warning.'
– Columnist Simon Heffer

'All the great writers of fiction for the young deal in shadows quite as much as in sun. Despite the Quidditch and the secrets in the dorm, Hogwarts is a dark place with a dark history, and so, for most of us, is childhood. These books are about life – the principal reason, I am sure, for their continuing success.'
– Writer, actor and director Julian Fellowes

— TRUE BRIT —

When Michael Newell took the director's chair for the film version of *Harry Potter And The Goblet Of Fire*, he was the first English director to shoot one of the series. The first two were directed by Chris Columbus, an American, while Alfonso Cuarón, the mastermind behind the third Harry Potter film, is Mexican.

— GOOD CAUSES —

JK Rowling has amassed a fortune by creating the Harry Potter phenomenon. Apart from gaining a reputation as a fabulous storyteller, she's also famous for her generosity to good causes. Here's a brief look at three of her favourites.

THE NATIONAL COUNCIL FOR ONE-PARENT FAMILIES

As well as being a contributor to the National Council for One-Parent Families, JK Rowling is also an ambassador for the charity (which means that she speaks for them in public whenever she can as well) and also works for the cause behind the scenes. When her marriage to Portuguese journalist Jorges Arantes collapsed, she retrieved her daughter from his flat and went to Edinburgh, where she fell into the bracket of 'one-parent family'.

She can still remember the daily dilemmas that being on one low income brought about: 'I remember reaching the supermarket checkout, counting out the money in coppers, finding out I was two pence short of a tin of baked beans and feeling I had to pretend I had mislaid a £10 note for the benefit of the bored girl at the till. Similarly unappreciated acting skills were required for my forays into Mothercare, where I would pretend to be examining clothes I could not afford for my daughter. At the time, I would be edging ever closer to the baby-changing room, where they offered a small supply of free nappies. And I hated relying on the kindness of relatives when it came to her new shoes.' Poverty, she says, is a lot like childbirth: 'You know that it's going to hurt before it happens, but you'll never know how much until you've experienced it.'

Six out of ten British families headed by a single parent live in poverty. Underlining her message about the joys of single motherhood, she asserts that her daughter was the best thing that ever happened to her, above even Harry Potter.

MS SOCIETY OF SCOTLAND

Multiple sclerosis affects an estimated 2,500,000 people worldwide. Sufferers are disabled when the body's immune system begins to attack the cells that protect the central nervous system (the brain and spinal cord). When this happens, the messages sent out by the brain are blocked or distorted so the body doesn't work as it should. MS usually occurs in people between 20 and 40 years of age, almost never developing in those under 12 or over 55. Nor does the disease follow a set pattern; for some people it brings about premature death while others with the disease manage to live an almost normal life. Three women for every two men suffer from MS. It's not hereditary and there's no known cure.

JK Rowling's mother died from multiple sclerosis at the age of 45, when the author herself was only 25. The loss of her mother at such a young age deeply affected her. When asked what she would wish to see in the Mirror of Erised, she spoke of a deep-rooted longing to spend just five more minutes with her mother, whom she yearns to tell about the grandchildren she's never seen and the successful book series she's never read. For this reason, JK is one of the benefactors of the MS Society of Scotland.

AMNESTY INTERNATIONAL
A worldwide organisation that campaigns for human rights, Amnesty International has more than 1.8 million members and supporters in over 150 different countries. Basically, its fundamental message is that human rights should be enjoyed by everyone on an equal basis and that they cannot be withdrawn for bad behaviour or curtailed for the purposes of controlling people's free will. The organisation has the following principles, taken from its website and slightly abbreviated:

- To free all prisoners of conscience
- To ensure a prompt and fair trial for all political prisoners
- To abolish the death penalty, torture and other cruel punishments
- To end extra-judicial executions and 'disappearances'
- To ensure that those who put themselves above the law are brought to justice.

The organisation was founded after a British lawyer was moved by the plight of two Portuguese students sentenced to a lengthy prison spell after raising a toast to freedom in 1961. After her time at university, JK Rowling worked for Amnesty International for some time.

— GOOD CAUSES (CONT'D) —

JK Rowling also joined an international campaign to halt the use of cage beds in psychiatric hospitals across Eastern Europe. These beds, fitted with metal bars or sturdy nets in order to imprison the mentally ill, have been in use in at least four countries for more than a century. Slovenia banned them in its hospitals several years ago.

Protestors including Rowling notched up a triumph in July 2004 when officials in Hungary and the Czech Republic agreed to scrap the use of such beds to contain people with behavioural difficulties. The decision came after sustained pressure was exerted by groups including the European Union and Amnesty International, which believes that the beds are both inhuman and degrading. For her part, Rowling appealed to the Czech Ambassador in Britain as well as Czech President Vaclav Klaus. Indeed, it was her appeal that swayed the health chief in the republic to act. Slovakia, however, has said that it will retain 654 cage beds for mentally or physically disabled patients. All four countries recently joined the EU.

OTHER

JK Rowling has also assisted the 999 Club, a charity that helps disadvantaged people in society to help themselves. In November 2004, a miniature book penned by her fetched £11,000 for the charity at a Sotheby's auction.

— MERCY, PERCY —

In the Harry Potter films, Chris Rankin, from Dereham, Norfolk, plays Percy Weasley, older brother of main player Ron. One of his most memorable moments was having his pocket soaked with toad wee as he carted the creature around during the filming of *Harry Potter And The Philosopher's Stone*. But how does he learn all his lines? 'I don't know how I do it, to be honest. It just happens: it goes in, I look at it and it's there.' Chris also helps to run a theatre company and appears regularly in panto.

— TWIN TALENTS —

JK Rowling grew up in the beautiful Forest of Dean, on the border between England and Wales, which was exactly the same picturesque area that popular playwright Dennis Potter called home. Potter the playwright (1935–94), the son of a coal miner, was born in Berry Hill, Coleford, Gloucestershire, and grew up with a fascination for books and words. In his career as a writer, he turned his hand to newspapers, plays, film manuscripts and novels, even at one time dabbling in politics. He believed that TV plays were just as artistically valid as those staged in a theatre and created a TV masterpiece, *The Singing Detective*, to prove it. Throughout his adult life, Potter suffered from a painful skin condition and ultimately died of pancreatic cancer.

— TEN THINGS YOU DIDN'T KNOW YOU — DIDN'T KNOW ABOUT JK ROWLING

1 She hates tripe, a dish made up of animal entrails.

2 She loves Hallowe'en and usually celebrates it by having a party.

3 She doesn't believe in magic.

4 Her favourite group is The Beatles.

5 Her favourite boy's name has always been Harry.

6 Her first story was written at the age of about six, in which the hero was a rabbit called Rabbit and the heroine was a giant bee called – you guessed it – Miss Bee. No marks for originality, then.

7 Although she's addicted to writing, she's never kept a diary for more than two weeks.

8 She hates watching herself on screen.

9 She loves the mad humour of Monty Python (a comedy group that rose to prominence in the '70s) and *The Simpsons*.

10 When she got her first job, as a bilingual secretary, her bosses were delighted to see her head bowed over sheets of paper, scribbling prolifically throughout the day. In fact, she was penning ideas for novels rather than tending to her day job – which made her, she claims, the worst secretary ever.

— NON-STARTERS —

Sometimes JK Rowling came up with book titles that ultimately failed to make the grade, while fans, journalists and mimics often derived book names that were imaginative but were…er…wrong, and some aspiring authors have used Harry Potter in the title of their books with another JK Rowling-esque phrase. Here's a selection of titles that have been tossed about regarding Harry Potter but have never seen the light of day. (Spot the ones that are obviously suggested in fun.)

Harry Potter And The Doomspell Tournament
Harry Potter And The Triwizard Tournament
Harry Potter And The Fortress Of Shadows
Harry Potter And The Green Flame Torch
Harry Potter And The Mountain Of Fantasy
Harry Potter And The Pillar Of Storge
Harry Potter And The Toenail Of Icklibogg
Harry Potter And The Enchanted Quill
Harry Potter And The Cup o' Hot Stuff

— HOW HARRY POTTER CHANGED MY LIFE —

'I needed to get out for my own sanity.'
– Chris Columbus, director of the first two Harry Potter films,
after his decision not to direct the third

'When it was announced that I was doing this *Harry Potter And The Prisoner Of Azkaban*, I was a superstar overnight at my kids' school.'
– Gary Oldman

'My life has changed surprisingly little. People come up to me and ask about the films, which is cool, and it's great to hear what they think about it all, but I do plenty of normal kids' stuff, like hanging out and having pizza parties.'
– Daniel Radcliffe

'The kids love the Harry Potter films so much, and I get lots of mail about it.'
– Julie Walters

'I guess the main things that have changed is that I get recognised and I've got an action figure of myself.'
– Emma Watson

'I never expected to be talking to journalists or doing lots of promotional work, and I have reached the point now where I have to say no to a lot of things just to make sure that I get enough time to write. On the other hand, I love travelling, and the chance to visit places I've never seen before is absolutely wonderful.'

– JK Rowling

'People don't recognise me at all. I walked past a group of people who had just watched the film the other day. They were discussing the scene at the end and they clocked me but they had no idea that they were talking about me.'

– Christian Coulson

'Whether I want to or not, I think I will be remembered for Harry Potter. But why not?'

– Jim Dale

'Harry Potter is my pension.'

– Maggie Smith

— 'HARRY POTTER MAKES ME SICK' —

Complaints by three *Harry Potter And The Order Of The Phoenix* readers of stress headaches has led a Washington doctor to highlight an all-new modern malady. Dr Howard Bennett, of the George Washington University Medical Center, identified 'Hogwarts headaches' among avid readers enjoying Rowling's hefty tome. In a letter to the *New England Journal Of Medicine*, Dr Bennett wrote, 'The presumed diagnosis for each child was a tension headache brought on by the effort required to plough through an 870-page book.' He went on to say that the cure – which is quite simply putting the book down – was rejected by two out of three patients.

Although his letter wasn't entirely serious, Dr Bennett did cite evidence about the growing size of Harry Potter books – from the 300-odd pages of the *Philosopher's Stone* to nearly three times that size by the time of the *Goblet Of Fire* – to predict a possible future dilemma: 'If this escalation continues as Rowling concludes the saga, there may be an epidemic of Hogwarts headaches in years to come.'

— JK ROWLING'S BOOKSHELF —

An avid reader since childhood, JK Rowling has often cited the novels that keep her bookshelf warm. Here, in no particular order, is a list of those books, what they're about and a word or two about their authors. Read each novel's first lines and see if you're hooked as she was.

MITFORD, JESSICA: *Hons And Rebels*
An autobiography of Mitford's early years.

Jessica Mitford (1917–96), also known as Decca, was one of six children born to Baron Redesdale and his wife. At home she was educated by governesses, and she and her sisters tried to make them quit as quickly as possible. On one occasion they wound a pet grass snake around the lavatory cord, causing the governess of the time to scream and faint. Two of her sisters were avid supporters of the Nazis while Decca preferred the politics of the Communist Party. Ultimately she ran away to Spain with her boyfriend, Esmond Romilly, a nephew of Sir Winston Churchill, but he was killed in 1941 after joining the Royal Canadian Air Force. Later she met and married radical lawyer Robert Treuhaft and both battled for civil rights in 1950s America in the face of overwhelming political opposition. Her bestselling book *The American Way Of Death*, written in 1963, was an exposé of the funeral industry. JK Rowling named her daughter for Jessica Mitford.

FIRST LINE: 'The Cotswold country, old and quaint, ridden with ghosts and legends, is today very much on the tourist route.'

NESBIT, E: *The Phoenix And The Carpet*
Five children find an old carpet, complete with odd-looking egg. The carpet can fly through time and space. The egg hatches into a phoenix that assists the youngsters during their ensuing adventures.

London-born Edith Nesbit (1858–1924) was educated in British boarding schools, as well as in France and Germany. After she married, she worked to maintain her children and her husband, who was often involved in failed business ventures. In 1884 she became a founder member of the Fabian

Society (sometimes she used the pen-name 'Fabian Bland'), an intellectual group that promoted socialism in Britain, and helped to form the Labour Party. Her other books include *The Railway Children, Five Children And It, The Story Of The Amulet, The Story Of The Treasure-seekers, The Wouldbegoods* and *The Enchanted Castle*. A lifelong smoker, she died of lung cancer.

FIRST LINE: 'It began with the day when it was almost the Fifth of November, and a doubt arose in some breast – Robert's, I fancy – as to the quality of the fireworks laid in for Guy Fawkes' celebration.'

LEWIS, CS: *The Lion, The Witch And The Wardrobe*
Four children evacuated from London during the Second World War discover that a wardrobe in a spare room of their new home leads to an exciting new world.

Belfast-born Clive Staples Lewis (1898–1963), known to his friends as 'Jack', became intrigued with mythology and legends after hearing the tales told to him by his Irish nurse. When he became an adult, he worked at both Oxford and Cambridge Universities, but he never forgot his fascination with all matters magical. A lifelong bachelor, he encountered children only at close quarters after some were evacuated to his household during the Second World War. Although he wrote other titles, including some for adults, he is chiefly remembered for his chronicles of Narnia, which actually begin with *The Magician's Nephew*, a scene-setter written after *The Lion, The Witch And The Wardrobe* about events that happened previously. When he was once asked why he wrote his children's books, he replied, 'People won't write the books I want, so I have to do it for myself.' One of his colleagues at university was JRR Tolkien, author of *The Hobbit* and The Lord Of The Rings trilogy.

FIRST LINE: 'Once there were four children whose names were Peter, Susan, Edmund and Lucy.'

GOUDGE, ELIZABETH: *The Little White Horse*
Orphan Maria Merryweather goes to Moonacre Manor to be cared for by her uncle, Sir Benjamin Merryweather. She

— JK ROWLING'S BOOKSHELF (CONT'D) —

finds her new world is full of misery and misunderstandings
that must be resolved before she once again sees the symbol
of perfect happiness: the little white horse.

The daughter of a clergyman, Elizabeth Goudge (1900–84) moved from the Somerset town of Wells to Ely in Cambridgeshire and finally to Oxford, where her father was a professor. Her first book, *The Fairies' Baby And Other Stories* (written in 1919), bombed. It was then 15 years before her second book, *Island Magic* – based on stories recalled by her mother, who was from Jersey – appeared in print. Then in 1946 she won the Carnegie Medal for *The Little White Horse*, while her book *Green Dolphin Country* was made into a film starring Lana Turner and Donna Reed. She was passionate about nature, once stating, 'Nothing living should ever be treated with contempt. Whatever it is that lives – a man, a tree, or a bird – should be touched gently because the time is short. "Civilisation" is another word for "respect for life".' Each year, the Elizabeth Goudge Trophy is awarded by the Romantic Novelists' Association in recognition of great and original writing.

FIRST LINE: 'The carriage gave another lurch and Maria Merryweather, Miss Heliotrope and Wiggins once more fell into each other's arms, sighed, gasped, righted themselves and fixed their attention upon those objects which were for each of them at this trying moment the source of courage and strength.'

GALLICO, PAUL: *The Snow Goose*
A hunchback artist and a girl join forces to look after wildlife.

His father was Italian and his mother was Austrian, but Paul Gallico (1897–1976) was an American, born in New York. He was a World War I veteran and newspaper journalist specialising in sport. A lifelong fan of boxing, he was once knocked out while sparring with world heavyweight champion Jack Dempsey. Later he gave up sports writing with the intention of devoting himself to fiction. In 1941, *The Snow Goose* was published to great acclaim, although soon afterwards he stopped writing stories for a few years to work as a war correspondent. Gallico loved fencing and fishing and was living in Antibes when he died.

FIRST LINE: 'The Great Marsh lies on the Essex coast between the village of Chelmbury and the ancient Saxon oyster-fishing hamlet of Wickaeldroth.'

SMITH, DODIE: *I Capture The Castle*
Teenage narrator relates the lives and times of her extraordinary family.

After her acting career foundered, Dodie Smith (1896–1990) worked as a buyer for the toy department of Heal's department store, where she met her future husband, Alex. The couple moved to America but sent food packages home to war-torn England and also visited people thrown into internment camps after America joined the Second World War in 1941. In 1943, their pet dalmatians had 15 puppies, one of which was stillborn but revived by Alex. The story was later included in her huge hit novel *One Hundred And One Dalmatians*, although her first book was *I Capture The Castle*, written in America but inspired by her homesickness for England.

FIRST LINE: 'I write this sitting in the kitchen sink.'

STREATFEILD, NOEL: *Ballet Shoes*
Orphans Pauline, Petrova and Posy Fossil are adopted by their Great-uncle Matthew, better known as GUM. When he disappears on a lengthy voyage, however, the children must pitch in with money-making schemes to help the family finances.

Although Noel Streatfeild (1895–1986) wrote no fewer than 58 books for children, *Ballet Shoes* was his first and most famous. The second of three daughters of a Sussex clergyman, Streatfeild worked in a munitions factory during World War One and then tried her luck as an actress, but it was writing that proved to be her special strength, inspired as it was by what she called her 'blotting-paper memory'.

FIRST LINE: 'The Fossils lived in the Cromwell Road.'

— JK ROWLING'S BOOKSHELF (CONT'D) —

BELLOC, HILAIRE: *Cautionary Tales For Children*
Innovative poetry that stands the test of time.

French-born Hilaire Belloc (1870–1953) fled to England with his family to escape the Franco-Prussian War. With his home near Paris laid waste, he made a new life for himself in England, even becoming an MP before becoming disillusioned with party politics. Although his grandfather was the famous radical Joseph Parkes, Belloc held surprisingly bigoted views and was firmly against women's right to vote. Nevertheless, he was a member of the Fabian Society for a while and campaigned against political corruption. Belloc lost one son in World War I and another in World War II. He was a prolific writer on all sorts of subjects, prompting one observer to call him 'the man who wrote a library', yet he is best remembered for his children's poetry, including 'Matilda', a poem about a little girl who told lies and was burned to death.

FIRST LINE: 'There was a boy whose name was Jim;
His friends were very good to him…'

FREUD, CLEMENT: 'Grimble'
A short story about a small boy of uncertain age with notoriously vague parents, who is left to fend for himself.

Grandson of famous psychologist Sigmund Freud and brother of artist Lucien Freud, Clement is famous as a writer, broadcaster and one-time politician. He is well known as having a passion for cookery and also for his contributions to the UK's Radio 4 show *Just A Minute*. Curiously, however, it was his appearance on advertisements for dog food that brought him his greatest celebrity renown, his hangdog expression making him ideal for the role.

FIRST LINE: 'This is about a boy called Grimble, who was about ten.'

AUSTEN, JANE: *Emma*
Pretty and smug, Emma Woodhouse enjoys organising the lives of those around her. However, her meddling threatens her personal happiness and she must learn to leave well alone.

Jane Austen (1775–1871) is one of England's most important novelists. One of eight children, she was especially close to her sister Cassandra, and was turning out novels by the age of 14, although her output came to a halt when her family moved to Bath and, later, Southampton. Only when she was back in the Hampshire countryside in which she had been born did her flow of words recommence. Among her other famous books are *Sense And Sensibility*, *Pride And Prejudice*, *Persuasion*, *Mansfield Park* and *Northanger Abbey*. She never married, died of a rare kidney disease and was buried in Winchester Cathedral.

FIRST LINE: 'Emma Woodhouse, handsome, clever and rich, with a comfortable home and happy disposition, seemed to unite some of the best blessings of existence and had lived nearly twenty-one years in the world with very little to distress or vex her.'

COLLINS, WILKIE: *The Moonstone*
A large yellow diamond swiped from an Indian shrine is presented to heroine Rachel Verrinder as a gift. However, the gem, cursed with bringing bad luck to its bearer, soon vanishes and a police sergeant gets on to the case. The mystery of its disappearance thickens considerably before being solved.

London-born William Wilkie Collins (1824–89) was the son of a painter. Although writing was his first love, Collins Jr also painted and once had a picture hung at the Royal Academy, and he counted Charles Dickens among his friends. His two most famous books were *The Woman In White* and *The Moonstone*, most of which he dictated while he was confined to bed with gout.

FIRST LINE: 'I address these lines – written in India – to my relations in England.'

DOYLE, RODDY: The Barrytown Trilogy
A teenager aims to alleviate the tedium of daily life on a run-down estate by getting a rock band together.

Before becoming a full-time writer, Roddy Doyle (1958–) was a secondary-school teacher in Dublin. He shot into the

— JK ROWLING'S BOOKSHELF (CONT'D) —

limelight when his first novel, *The Commitments*, was turned into a film that became famous largely for its soundtrack. This book forms the first instalment of the Barrytown trilogy, which follows the fortunes (or otherwise) of the Rabbitte family, the other two books being *The Snapper* and *The Van*. Doyle is reluctant to advise budding authors on what to do, stating, 'If writers want to write, they want to write and they should be left alone. I am no mentor and I don't think I'd be doing anyone any favours if I said, "Come on, let's do it this way." We'll leave the cloning to the sheep.'

First line: —We'll ask Jimmy, said Outspan. —Jimmy'll know.

DE BERNIÈRES, LOUIS: *Captain Corelli's Mandolin*
When Italians invade the Greek island of Cephalonia during the Second World War, one of the soldiers falls in love with the doctor's daughter, Pelagia, but an idyllic romance is coloured by the conflict.

Before making it big as an author, Louis de Bernières had a range of jobs, including car mechanic and landscape gardener. He also taught English in Colombia, and he consequently wrote three novels set in South America. His fourth novel, *Captain Corelli's Mandolin*, published in 1994, was his first major hit and was later turned into a film starring Nicolas Cage. Since then he has written short stories, plays and another novel: *Birds Without Wings*.

FIRST LINE: 'Dr Iannis had enjoyed a satisfactory day in which none of his patients had died or got any worse.'

DICKENS, CHARLES: *A Tale Of Two Cities*
A story of love, loss, loyalty, morality and self-sacrifice set against the backdrop of the French Revolution.

Charles Dickens (1812–70) was scarred in childhood by the experience of wrapping bottles in a blacking factory after his father was thrown into jail for debt. The experience gave him a lifelong passion for social justice and shaped him as a compulsive worker, often adopting the pseudonym 'Boz'. He achieved considerable fame during his lifetime with novels such as *Oliver Twist*, *David Copperfield* and *Great Expectations*. Much of his work appeared in newspapers in weekly instalments, and he was well known for giving public readings.

FIRST LINE: 'It was the best of times, it was the worst of times, it was the age of wisdom, it was the age of foolishness, it was the epoch of belief, it was the epoch of incredulity, it was the season of Light, it was the season of Darkness, it was the spring of hope, it was the winter of despair, we had everything before us, we had nothing before us, we were all going direct to Heaven, we were all going direct the other way – in short, the period was so far like the present period that some of its noisiest authorities insisted on its being received, for good or for evil, in the superlative degree of comparison only.'

— FILM MAGIC —

In his scenes with Dobby during the making of the second Harry Potter film, actor Daniel Radcliffe had to talk to an orange ball on the end of a stick representing the house elf. The unearthly image of Dobby – a self-abuser who was tormented by the Malfoys – was added later with computer technology. Radcliffe's greatest challenge was to ensure that he kept his eyes in line with a single spot on the ball so that it appeared he was talking directly to the humble house elf.

— STAR QUALITY —

Some film stars seem to have been born under lucky stars. Others, however, create their own good fortune through hard work. The second category includes Rupert Grint, who has become one of the world's best-known child actors after starring in the Harry Potter films as Ron Weasley. When he found out that auditions were taking place for roles in the first Harry Potter film, after watching a children's news show, he knuckled down. 'I did my own video with me, first of all, pretending to be my drama teacher, who unfortunately was a girl. Then I did a rap of how I wanted to be Ron, and then I made my own script up and sent it off.' After leaving other hopefuls eating his dust, he hasn't looked back since.

— HARRY POTTER TIMELINE —

1990   Harry Potter is thought up by JK Rowling on a train journey between London and Manchester. She begins writing *Harry Potter And The Philosopher's Stone* that night.

1991   Following the death of her mother, JK Rowling moves to Portugal, taking with her the ever-expanding Harry Potter manuscript.

1994   Rowling returns to Britain with daughter Jessica and an even bigger version of Harry Potter.

1995   Rowling finds an agent for the completed manuscript.

1996   Bloomsbury agree to publish.

1997   June: *Harry Potter And The Philosopher's Stone* is published by Bloomsbury.

   July: Manuscript of *Harry Potter And The Chamber Of Secrets* is submitted to Bloomsbury.

   November: *Harry Potter And The Philosopher's Stone* wins the Nestlé Smarties Gold Award (9–11 Years category).

1998   February: *Harry Potter And The Philosopher's Stone* becomes the Children's Book of the Year Award at the British Book Awards.

   July: *Harry Potter And The Chamber Of Secrets* is released in hardback in the UK and, five months later, wins its author the Nestlé Smarties Gold Award in the 9–11 Years category for the second year running. JK Rowling is the first author to achieve a back-to-back triumph for the award.

   October: *Harry Potter And The Philosopher's Stone* is published in the US by Scholastic under the title *Harry Potter And The Sorcerer's Stone*. Warner Bros secures the film rights for the first two Harry Potter books.

1999   January: *Harry Potter And The Chamber Of Secrets* appears in paperback.

   July: *Harry Potter And The Prisoner Of Azkaban* comes out in hardback.

December: JK Rowling receives a special award after winning the Nestlé Smarties Gold Award for the third year in succession.

2000   February: *Harry Potter And The Prisoner Of Azkaban* wins the Whitbread Children's Book of the Year Award.

April: *Harry Potter And The Prisoner Of Azkaban* comes out in paperback.

June: JK Rowling is awarded an OBE.

July: *Harry Potter And The Goblet Of Fire* comes out in hardback.

2001   March: Two books on the Hogwarts theme are published to raise cash for Comic Relief.

July: *Harry Potter And The Goblet Of Fire* is published in paperback.

November: *Harry Potter And The Philosopher's Stone* film is released.

2002   November: *Harry Potter And The Chamber Of Secrets* film is released.

2003   April: *Harry Potter And The Chamber Of Secrets* DVD is released.

June: *Harry Potter And The Goblet Of Fire* is published in a synchronised operation with the States.

2004   June: *Harry Potter And The Prisoner Of Azkaban* film is released.

2005   July: *Harry Potter And The Half-Blood Prince* is unleashed on a Potter-hungry public after advance orders for the book reach record levels.

November: The film version of *Harry Potter And The Goblet Of Fire* is released into cinemas.

— FORTY-YEAR FRIENDSHIP —

Although actor Michael Gambon had the difficult job of being a replacement Dumbledore in the film version of *Harry Potter And The Prisoner Of Azkaban* following the death of Richard Harris, he felt among friends as soon as he arrived on the set. After all, he had known Maggie Smith (better known to Harry Potter fans as Professor McGonagall) for no fewer than 40 years.

— THINKING SMALL —

The appearance of (fake) talkative shrunken heads in the third Harry Potter film was the brainwave of director Alfonso Cuarón, although JK Rowling admits to wishing she'd thought of it first.

Spookily, there's still an Amazonian tribe of headhunters in the business of producing the real thing. The Shuar tribesmen, part of the Jivaro clan, have for years been doing unspeakable things to severed heads, as they celebrate Hallowe'en all year round.

The details of manufacturing a shrunken head are too gruesome to go into here, and the end product is itself chilling. Suffice to say that there's no way a real shrunken head can talk, as the lips are sewn together. Nevertheless, these revolting artefacts are highly sought after, and a roaring trade in shrunken heads has been good news for the Shuar Indians' economy – and bad news for their enemies.

— MAGIC CIRCLE —

Emma Watson has starred in all the Harry Potter films released so far, as has Rupert Grint, who was also in the movie *Thunderpants* with the narrator of the Harry Potter tapes in Britain, Stephen Fry, who also starred in a made-for-TV version of author Mervyn Peake's *Gormenghast* with Zoë Wanamaker, who is a US citizen, like the director of the first two Harry Potter films, Chris Columbus, who is a big fan of *Monty Python's Flying Circus*, which featured John Cleese, who was in the James Bond film *The World Is Not Enough* alongside Robbie Coltrane, once a comedian in the Comic Strip series of films with Dawn French, who likes to live it large, as does Miriam Margoyles, who also starred in an adaptation of *The Phoenix And The Carpet*, written by E Nesbit, who is a favourite author of JK Rowling, whose mother died of multiple sclerosis, as did the heroine of the film *Duet For One*, played by Frances de la Tour, three times winner at the prestigious Sir Laurence Olivier Theatre Awards, one of which was won by Richard Harris and one by his successor as Dumbledore, Michael Gambon, who starred in the film *Gosforth Park* with Maggie Smith, who played Betsey Trotwood in the 1999 TV film *David Copperfield*, which had as one of its stars Daniel Radcliffe, who also starred in

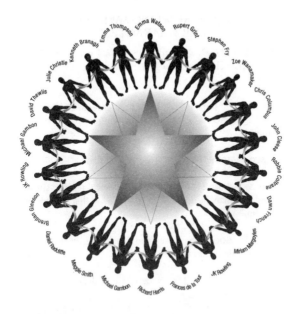

The Tailor Of Panama with Brendan Gleeson, who starred in *The Snapper*, a film of the book by Roddy Doyle (cited by JK Rowling as another favourite author), which was made in 1993 and set in Dublin, the birthplace of Michael Gambon, who starred in *Endgame* with David Thewlis, who was in *Dragonheart* alongside Julie Christie, who came out of retirement to play Gertrude in the 1996 film *Hamlet*, which starred and was directed by Kenneth Branagh, who was once married to Emma Thompson, who shares the same first name and birthday (15 April) as Emma Watson.

— WITCH DATE 6 —

Dumbledore achieved fame in 1945 for defeating the evil wizard Grindelwald, if his chocolate frog trading card is to be believed. In the Muggle world, this was, of course, the year in which the Allies defeated Nazi Germany and other Axis powers. Presumably, Albus Dumbledore represents Britain on this occasion and Grindelwald Germany under Hitler.

— WHAT JK ROWLING SAYS ABOUT — HER CHARACTERS

HERMIONE: 'She's a lot like me when I was younger. I wasn't that clever but I was definitely that annoying at times.'

HERMIONE: 'I hope it is clear that underneath Hermione's swottiness there is a lot of insecurity and a great fear of failure.'

DRACO MALFOY: 'He does have a certain flair.'

PROFESSOR LUPIN: 'Although he's wonderful teacher and a wonderful man, he does like to be liked, and that's where he slips up.'

LUNA LOVEGOOD: 'She is prepared to believe 1,000 made-up things before breakfast.'

DOLORES UMBRIDGE: 'I really loathe Umbridge.'

PROFESSOR MCGONAGALL: 'She's a bit of an old softy.'

GILDEROY LOCKHART: 'He's the only character deliberately based on a real person – but I have to say that the living model was worse. He was a shocking man.'

RITA SKEETER: 'She is loathsome – morally, she's horrible – but I can't help admiring her toughness.'

SEVERUS SNAPE: 'Professor Snape is a lot like one of my old teachers, but I'm not saying which one.'

SIRIUS BLACK: 'Sirius is very good at spouting bits of personal philosophy, but he doesn't always live up to them.'

LORD VOLDEMORT: 'The most evil wizard for hundreds and hundreds of years.'

WINKY: 'She'll never be entirely cured of her Butterbeer addiction.'

— THE BEST OF TIMES... —

JK Rowling once wrote a Harry Potter chapter that didn't need the wholesale revision she normally devotes to her work. 'I remember vividly the afternoon. My daughter fell asleep and I ran into the café on a beautifully sunny day. I sat down and I wrote that chapter from beginning to end. I think I changed two words. That's very unusual for me.'

— AND THE WORST OF TIMES... —

Generally, JK Rowling is her own worst critic, once going on record as saying, 'There's a chapter in book four that I rewrote 13 times, and at one point I thought, "The book will never happen if I keep rewriting chapter whatever-it-was."'

— HARRY POTTER'S BROKEN RECORDS —

Harry Potter And The Half-Blood Prince is the fastest selling book of all time. Within 24 hours of its launch, more than 2 million copies were sold in the UK while in the US the figure was a mighty 6.8 million. Add in the sales garnered in a further 13 countries and the figure comes to an estimated 10 million. Indeed, experts decided that the sixth Potter book sold more in a day than Dan Brown's bestseller *The Da Vinci Code* sold in a year. The wizarding novel was so popular that British booksellers WH Smith claimed to have sold 13 copies every second in that first frantic day of sale.

In 2001, the first Harry Potter film broke box-office records on both sides of the Atlantic, taking £16 million in ticket sales in the UK and a massive $90.3 million (£60 million) in the States during its first weekend. In Britain, the previous movie receipts record-holder was *Star Wars: Episode I – The Phantom Menace*, which took £9.2 million during its first weekend in cinemas. In America, *Harry Potter And The Sorceror's Stone* got the better of *Jurassic Park*, which had taken £50 million in its opening weekend.

When it opened in 500 UK cinemas on 31 May 2004, the movie *Harry Potter And The Prisoner Of Azkaban* took £5.3 million in a single day, more than the initial opening receipts from the first and second films put together. On its release in America, it was screened in 3,855 movie theatres and took a record-breaking $40.8 million in a day.

Two months after the third Harry Potter film came out, *Harry Potter And The Order Of The Phoenix* was published in paperback and sold 1.7 million copies in just 24 hours. After its predecessor, *Harry Potter And The Goblet Of Fire,* sold 3 million copies in the first 48 hours, *Publishers Weekly* dubbed it 'the fastest selling book in history'.

In America, 5 million copies of *Harry Potter And The Order Of The Phoenix* were sold in the first 24 hours of the book going on sale, according to publishers Scholastic, beating the record set by *Harry Potter And The Goblet Of Fire.* According to internet booksellers Amazon.com, 350,000 advance orders were received for *Harry Potter And The Order Of The Phoenix*, more than for any other book in its history. The orders came from places as far-flung as Nepal, Tanzania and Fiji.

In April 2003, the DVD of *Harry Potter And The Chamber Of Secrets* became the fastest selling in Britain after 1,012,000 copies were sold in two days. In the US, meanwhile, the DVD and video release of the film notched up £90 million after 6 million copies were sold in a single day.

When *Harry Potter And The Order Of The Phoenix* sold 1 million copies on its launch day in June 2003, it became the fastest selling book in British history.

When *Harry Potter And The Goblet Of Fire* was turned into a movie, it became the most expensive of all time, costing an estimated £171 million.

Published on 21 June 2003, *Harry Potter And The Order Of The Phoenix* had the largest first-edition print run in history, with no fewer than 8.5 million copies being produced for the day.

Harry Potter And The Half-Blood Prince is the first novel to be published simultaneously in Braille and large print, giving equal access at last to blind readers and the partially sighted.

In the seven-year spell between 1998 and 2005, JK Rowling was the UK's bestselling fiction author.

— THE WRONG HAT —

On the advice of pals, JK Rowling logged on to an unofficial HP site that offered an on-line sorting hat service. The author was taken aback when she was sorted against expectations into Hufflepuff house. 'I wasn't that pleased,' she confessed later. 'Obviously I'm supposed to be Gryffindor. If anyone's Gryffindor I'm supposed to be Gryffindor.'

The sorting hat, of course, is the device by which new pupils are channelled into Hogwart's houses. It is both poetic and wise and hints at possessing amazing foresight into the future when it issues warnings about upcoming events, especially in *Harry Potter And The Order Of The Phoenix*.

In the first two Harry Potter films the lyrical sorting hat is voiced by veteran actor Leslie Phillips some sixty years after he made his big screen debut debut. (He was a bit part actor in the 1938 film *Lassie from Lancashire*.) He became famous for depicting plummy-voiced lovable rogues in the 'Carry On' series of films, which were slapstick comedies produced mostly in the Sixties. Co-incidentally, in the 1960 movie *Carry on Constable* his role was as PC Tom Potter. He also appeared in the hit film *Lara Croft: Tomb Raider* in the same year *Harry Potter And The Philosopher's Stone* was released – the year he celebrated his 77th birthday. A keen Spurs fan, Phillips was awarded an OBE in 1998.

— CREATIVE TENSION —

Quidditch is a violent, tactical, energetic sport that requires a clear mind and an agile body, but just how did JK come up with something so unlike anything else? She has revealed it came forth from her fervid imagination after she'd had a row with a boyfriend and stormed off to the local pub.

— LUCKY JIM —

When Jamie Waylett won the on-screen part of Vincent Crabbe in the Harry Potter films, anyone would be forgiven for thinking he was a fortunate fella. In fact, it was a marked change of luck for Jamie, who once nearly died after being hit by a car. He was unconscious and in intensive care for three days after the accident, and his parents were told that the chances of him making a full recovery were slim. Just when it seemed the outlook was bleakest, however, a family friend asked doctors to try a new approach. The result was a blood transfusion, after which Jamie began to show almost immediate signs of improvement. Within a year, he was back at school – in time for a surprise visit by the casting directors…

— CHILD CRUELTY —

JK Rowling's name is pronounced *roll-ing*, as in 'rolling stone', rather than *row-ling*, like 'howling'. When she taught French for a short spell while awaiting the publication of the first Harry Potter book, her students taunted her by singing the first line of the theme song to the US Western series *Rawhide*, which goes, 'Rollin', rollin', rollin'/Though the streams are swollen/Keep them dogies rollin', rawhide...'

When it comes to pronunciation, Rowling gave her arch-villain a challenging name, like her own. The correct way to say it is as if the last letter was silent – ie *Voldemore*.

— WITCH DATE 7 —

After 1965, when the Ban on Experimental Breeding of Magical Creatures was passed into wizarding law, the creation of new and terrible monsters was outlawed, thus saving the human race from witnessing some terrible sights.

In any event, Muggles were far too absorbed with their own news items at the time to notice any magical goings-on. In the same year, Soviet cosmonaut Aleksei Leonov became the first man to walk in space, while the first US combat troops were sent to South Vietnam and the Mont Blanc tunnel through the Alps was opened. Meanwhile, two musical phenomena – The Beatles and Elvis Presley – met for the first and only time.

— CHALLENGING TIMES —

Every year hundreds of new books are published, and every year there are readers who are offended or upset by what they read between the covers of some of them. Some people even try to get books banned, and it's for this reason that the American Library Association keeps a record of the most challenged books of 1990 to 2000. In a charted result of 6,364 challenges, JK Rowling's series comes in at number seven, reflecting a fairly hefty number of complaints in the US about the content of the Harry Potter books. Here's a list of the top ten most challenged books, as published by the American Library Association.

1. Scary Stories (series) by Alvin Schwartz
2. *Daddy's Roommate* by Michael Willhoite
3. *I Know Why The Caged Bird Sings* by Maya Angelou
4. *The Chocolate War* by Robert Cormier
5. *The Adventures Of Huckleberry Finn* by Mark Twain
6. *Of Mice And Men* by John Steinbeck
7. Harry Potter (series) by JK Rowling
8. *Forever* by Judy Blume
9. *Bridge To Terabithia* by Katherine Paterson
10. Alice (series) by Phyllis Reynolds Naylor

The placing puts the number of concerns expressed about Harry Potter ahead of books like those in the Goosebumps series (number 16), *The Witches* by Roald Dahl (number 27), *To Kill A Mockingbird* by Harper Lee (number 41), *Curses, Hexes And Spells* by Daniel Cohen (number 73) and *Mommy Laid An Egg* by Babette Cole (number 82).

The ALA takes its statistics from two sources, newspapers and reports, and compiles the annual results in a database. In its assessment of challenges covering 2003 alone, the Harry Potter series came in higher still, at number two, for its references to wizardry and magic. If that wasn't enough, JK Rowling was also one of the most frequently challenged authors in 2002, 2001 and 2000.

The ALA is concerned that a volley of complaints will lead to censorship. On its website, it admits that complaints are usually made with noble motives: 'Books usually are challenged with the best intentions – to protect others, frequently children, from difficult ideas and information.' Actually, it is most likely to be parents who make the complaints. Nevertheless, the ALA believes that banning books – and, much worse, burning them – will deprive people of their right to free expression. As a consequence, they host an event known as 'Banned Books Week', in which people are urged to read books cloaked in controversy. As the ALA's website explains, 'The positive message of "Banned Books Week: Free People Read Freely" is that, due to the commitment of librarians, teachers, parents, students and other concerned citizens, most challenges are unsuccessful and most materials are retained in the school curriculum or library collection.'

— THE END —

The final chapter of Harry Potter VII, the as yet unnamed final book in the series charting the life of Harry Potter at Hogwarts, has already been written and lies in a secret, safe place, where it will remain until the chapters preceding it are complete.

— PUPPET LOVE? —

A Russian lawyer threatened to sue Harry Potter filmmakers after claiming that the cinema depiction of Dobby the house elf was based on the image of Russian president Vladimir Putin. There are, however, clear differences between the two, besides the not insignificant fact that one is a studio-made puppet while the other is a senior statesman. For instance, one has a big nose and goggly eyes and is often tongue-tied while Dobby is a veritable chatterbox. To his credit, Putin refused to comment on the likeness, yet some outraged Russians nevertheless wanted to magic up a courtroom brawl with the filmmakers.

They might, in fact, have had a point. On the BBC's website, a poll run on the CBBC page asked people if they thought that Dobby looked like Putin. No fewer than 63 per cent thought that the humble house elf was a dead ringer for the Russian leader.

— TOP TIPS —

Few writers have made it as big as JK Rowling, although there are plenty of potential authors out there wanting to write a successful book of their own. For them she offers this guidance: 'I doubt a writer who has got what it takes will need me to tell them this, but – persevere!'

For budding book illustrators, the artist behind the Harry Potter book covers, Mary GrandPré, also has some sound advice: 'The combination of a good basic understanding of what makes a picture work – good composition, good colour, good drawing – combined with a strong concept can enable you to work on anything.'

— DIVINATION CLASSES —

Hermione's least favourite lesson is Divination, taught by the highly melodramatic Professor Trelawney. Hermione's suspicion is that, rather than being the most difficult of the magic arts, as Trelawney claims, it is actually the most ludicrous. Dumbledore concedes that prediction is 'a very difficult business indeed'.

Divining the future is certainly a talent that people have yearned to acquire through the ages. There are literally scores of methods that have been tried but whose accuracy has never been proven. If you want to work out how best to peer into forthcoming events, you might find the following bluffers' guide to divination helpful.

READING TEA LEAVES

Properly known as *tasseomancy*, this is the interpretation of the detritus left in the bottom of a tea cup after the beverage has been slurped. Tea has been drunk for centuries, and tea-leaf reading probably originated among the Chinese, some of the earliest tea drinkers. With the fashion for spiritualism in the 18th and 19th centuries in the West there came an increasing popularity for tea-leaf readings, assisted by nomadic gypsies who claimed to be masters in the art. The practice requires the drinker to turn out his or her cup remains onto a saucer so that the reader can search for tell-tale patterns and images. Alas, the boom in tea bags has put tasseomancy into decline, to be replaced by *coffeography*, the reading of coffee grounds. If you do find yourself staring at some well-

— DIVINATION CLASSES (CONT'D) —

placed dregs, look out for the shape of a horseshoe (indicating good luck), a kite (symbolising ambitions) and a hand (meaning help is around the corner).

YARROW STICKS
In ancient China, a long-held belief in a complex system known as I Ching is rooted in the results gained from tossing 56 yarrow sticks and noting the patterns into which they fall. This practice has spiritual, ritual and religious significance for the Chinese, but many Westerners find it hard to fathom .

PALMISTRY

It doesn't take a genius to work out that this is all about reading the lines and bumps on the inner hand, whereby the reader is able to determine character and destiny after careful scrutiny of the subject's palm. The practice was popular during medieval times, although it was soon banned by the Church, who saw it as a form of witchcraft. It regained popularity, however, during the golden age of spiritualism in the late 19th and early 20th centuries. Most experienced palm readers maintain that predictions derived from this practice are dependent on the actions of the individual and that palm patterns can be changed as life events unfold.

ENTRAILS
In ancient times, self-confessed seers believed that they could predict the future by looking at the innards of dead animals or even humans. This sounds deeply disgusting, but it does remind me of that very old joke about the twin founders of Rome, Romulus and Remus, where Romulus asks, 'Why did the sacred chicken cross the road?' and Remus replies, 'I don't know. Let's cut it open and find out.'

CRYSTAL BALL

Crystal-ball gazers come armed with a small transparent globe that appears, to the untrained eye, as either clear or perhaps a little misty. (This is presumably behind the title of the Hogwarts-approved textbook *Unfogging The Future*.) After immense trance-like concentration, the gazer will see visions and colours that indicate what's going to occur in the coming weeks. The aim for the reader is to reach into their inner self and pull up thoughts that they weren't even aware of having. Another word for the process is *scrying*, from the old English word *descry*, meaning 'to succeed in discerning'.

ORACLES

To consult an oracle is to parley with a supernatural being, usually through a human medium. Oracles are believed to know everything, so they are an ideal source of advice. Alas, the priests, prophets or witch doctors charged with divining the oracular can be dodgy, so the 'wisdom' is often skewed.

TAROT CARDS

Although it looks similar to a deck of ordinary playing cards, a pack of tarot cards is radically different. For a start, there are 78 of them, divided into two parts: the Major Arcana and the Minor Arcana (*arcana* meaning secret or mysterious). The Major Arcana – also known as *trumps* – consists of 22 numbered picture cards, each of which has a different meaning depending on its position when it is dealt. The Minor Arcana, meanwhile, is split into four suits, like ordinary playing cards, although each suit contains 14 cards. The names of the suits are 'swords' (indicating ill fortune), 'pentacles' (linked to material success), 'wands' (connected to work) and 'cups' (associated with love and good fortune). Tarot cards have a long history but were linked to divination only after the 18th century.

— DIVINATION CLASSES (CONT'D) —

DREAMS

Harry is often troubled by dreams that appear so real that he feels he's flown out of his bed and is actually at the scene he's envisaging. He's not alone in experiencing this kind of nocturnal vision. Almost everyone has had a dream at some stage in their lives that seems real and appears to signify something important. Indeed, in ancient times people put great store by the interpretation of dreams. Then, in the 20th century, eminent psychiatrists decided that dreams indicate what lies in the subconscious mind. There are still many who believe that dreams can be a form a telepathic communication, which means that they are a glimpse of future events or even that one person is sending a message to another via the dream world. There is also a phenomenon known as *lucid dreaming*, where someone who is asleep recognises that they are in the middle of a dream.

DOWSING

Dowsing involves using sticks, a pendulum or even a bent wire coathanger to determine the whereabouts of water, gold or dead bodies. As the dowser walks over the object they are looking for, the instrument they're using dips or trembles to indicate the desired object's presence. No one knows why dowsing works, and at times the practice has been branded demonic or downright crazy. However, today dowsers are frequently called in on farms, building projects or archaeological digs, particularly to seek out water courses.

NUMEROLOGY
As its name implies, numerology is rooted in the study of numbers and is based on the belief that certain numerical values equate to events and character traits.

ARITHMANCY
This is a skill that was honed by the Ancient Greeks and Chaldeans (one-time residents of what is now southern Iraq), who placed their 21-letter alphabet into groups that were linked to planets. By careful study of the stars, they imagined that they could foretell the future. Such was their reputation as stargazers that the Romans knew the Chaldeans as excellent astronomers.

RUNES
Runes look like a kind of alphabet and are firmly rooted in mysticism, being used to express not just words but also futures and fortunes. Runic symbols were spread all over Europe and beyond by the well-travelled Vikings and are hence associated with Scandinavian communities; indeed, the Nordic god Odin is said to have gained secret wisdom from them. We don't know much about the period in history in which the Vikings launched their campaigns of conquest, known as the Dark Ages, but we do know that runic symbolism was rife at that time. Only when the Christian Church embarked on a campaign to stamp out paganism during the Middle Ages did free usage of runes die out. However, they made a comeback in Germany in the late 19th century when one man, Siegfried Adolf Kunner, fashioned his body in rune-shaped positions while yodelling in order to release inner magic. This trend didn't catch on, but runes made a later appearance in Nazi Germany, as the Swastika and other Nazi insignia were adopted from the runic alphabet. Small rune stones, each marked with an individual symbol, are sometimes used in fortune-telling.

— DIVINATION CLASSES (CONT'D) —

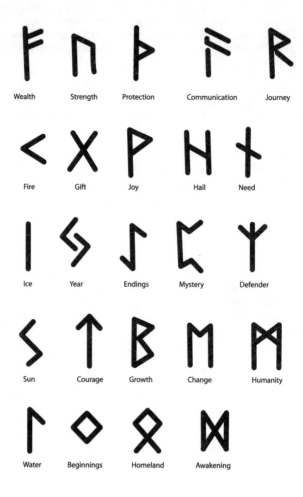

Wealth	Strength	Protection	Communication	Journey
Fire	Gift	Joy	Hail	Need
Ice	Year	Endings	Mystery	Defender
Sun	Courage	Growth	Change	Humanity
Water	Beginnings	Homeland	Awakening	

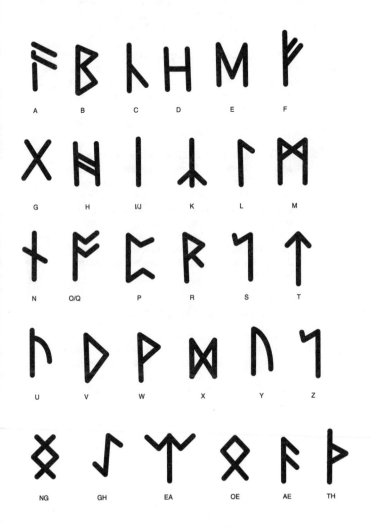

— HEAD START —

Harry Potter and company have been awarded one accolade usually reserved only for the great and the good in real life: in Australia their images grace an issue of stamps that has become seriously collectable. In an edition of ten different 50c stamps, the heads of Harry, Hermione, Ron, Professors Dumbledore, McGonagall, Snape and Lupin, Draco Malfoy, Hagrid and Sirius Black adorn the collection. If you want a souvenir stamp sheet and you can't get to an Australian post office to purchase them, try the relevant page at the Australian Post Office's website: www.auspost.com.au/stamps.

— JO'S HERO —

On Boxing Day 2001, JK Rowling married Dr Neil Murray, a graduate of Glasgow University's medical school. When they first met, he'd read only ten pages of her first book and was largely unaware of how popular Rowling had become. While friends were delighted that she seemed to have found love with a man four years her junior, they couldn't help but notice that bespectacled Murray – who has short, dark, spiky hair – is a dead ringer for her wizard hero, Harry.

— PLANE MADNESS —

After inspiration for the names of the Hogwarts houses struck her, JK Rowling made a note of them on the first piece of paper to hand: an airline sick bag. Even after the names Gryffindor, Hufflepuff, Ravenclaw and Slytherin became etched into the memory of every child in Britain, she kept the sick bag as a memento.

— EARLY RETIREMENT —

The manuscript for *Harry Potter And The Philosopher's Stone* was completed a year before JK Rowling found a willing publisher. When Bloomsbury eventually agreed to print the book in 1996, she says, it was one of the best moments of her life. Within a few months, the American publishing company Scholastic bought the publishing rights, giving Rowling sufficient cash to give up teaching in favour of pursuing a full-time career as a writer.

— IT'S A BUG'S LIFE —

Mary GrandPré has become famous for her illustrations of the Harry Potter storylines that appear in the US editions of Rowling's books. What isn't so widely known is that she was one of the team that developed the scenery for the animated film *Antz*, starring the voice of Woody Allen. To do so she had to get an ant's-eye view of the world and was constantly using a giant magnifying glass to see how ordinary, everyday objects would appear to a tiny creature.

— LOST IN TRANSLATION —

In an attempt to cash in on the success of *Harry Potter And The Order Of The Phoenix*, a writer in Venezuela translated the English version five months before the official Spanish edition was published. Not only was the book illegal but it was also littered with errors and apologies from the translator, who didn't understand JK Rowling's colloquial English.

On one page the unknown translator warns readers, 'Here comes something that I'm unable to translate. Sorry,' while another page reads, '"You gave him the old one-two." (I'm sorry, I didn't understand what that meant.)' There are numerous other mistakes for which the author apologises in notes at the front of the book.

Although the cover is an exact replica of the English edition, this illicit South American book has fewer pages. Two people were arrested and charged with producing the copies.

— STAGE FRIGHT —

A rumour that she had appeared or planned to appear in one of the Harry Potter films was firmly quashed by JK Rowling, who admitted that she was requested to do so by the filmmakers, who wanted her to appear as Lily Potter, as seen through the Mirror of Erised. She turned down the opportunity, confessing, 'I wasn't cut out to be an actress,

— STAGE FRIGHT (CONT'D) —

even one who just has to stand there and wave. I would have messed it up somehow.'

— EIGHT-LEGGED FREAKS —

Tolerant and broad-minded though she is, there's one thing that JK Rowling can't stand: spiders. As if to underline just how miserable Harry's existence was with the Dursleys, she tells us that the cupboard under the stairs where he lived at their house was filled with them. For her, writing the scene in the *Chamber Of Secrets* featuring giant arachnids was the stuff of nightmares. Rupert Grint, too, has confessed that he is also a spider-hater.

Despite the fact that out of some 40,000 different kinds of spiders only about 30 are poisonous, and that you're more likely to be killed by a champagne cork than you are by a spider, JK and Rupert aren't alone in their fear of spiders; indeed, arachnophobia (the medical term for their condition) is the world's most common fear. For the literally minded, a full chart of the world's top-ten fears, complete with their relevant Latin terms, is listed below:

1. Arachnophobia (spiders)
2. Sociophobia (people and social situations)
3. Aerophobia (flying)
4. Agoraphobia (open spaces)
5. Claustrophobia (confined spaces)
6. Emetophobia (vomiting)
7. Altophobia (heights)
8. Carcinophobia (cancer)
9. Brontophobia (thunderstorms)
10. Necrophobia (death)

(Source: *Top Ten Of Everything* by Russell Ash)

— MY WORD! —

Harry Potter And The Order Of The Phoenix is some 70,000 words longer than the New Testament. However, author JK Rowling still has some ground to make up, sales-wise, on the good book. To date, the Bible has sold more than 66 billion copies while, although undeniably popular, all the Harry Potter books combined have sold just 260 million. Indeed, the Harry Potter publishing phenomenon has some way to go before it catches even former Chinese leader Mao Tse Tung's *Little Red Book*, which has sold 800 million copies.

— SCORE DRAW —

Harry Potter might be ace at Quidditch, but he's not so hot on the more usual schoolboy pastime of soccer. Actor Daniel Radcliffe confesses he hardly ever kicks a football, although he is a supporter of Fulham FC – the Premier Division club nearest his home – which is owned by businessman and Harrods store owner Mohammed al-Fayed.

— HARRY POTTER, CHART-TOPPER —

A survey conducted by the Prince of Wales Arts and Kids Foundation in Britain discovered that Harry Potter was top of the charts, as far as children were concerned. In the 2004 survey, 300 young people aged between 7 and 14 were questioned about their favourite books, and Harry Potter came out in the number-one spot. More than half named a Harry Potter book in their top-three best reads. Most of the popular works of fiction have been the subject of a screen adaptation. The top ten was as follows:

BESTSELLERS

Top 10 Books

	Title	Author
1	Harry Potter	JK Rowling
2	The Lord of the Rings	JRR Tolkien
3	Charlie and the Chocolate Factory	Roald Dahl
4	The Cat in the Hat	Dr Seuss
5	Matilda	Roald Dahl
6	The Twits	Roald Dahl
7	Trace Beaker books	Jaqueline Wilson
8	The Jungle Book	Rudyard Kipling
9	The BFG	Roald Dahl
10	Winnie the Pooh	AA Milne

— WHO IS THE REAL HEDWIG? —

We all know that Hedwig is Harry's beloved owl, but, like other names used by JK Rowling, Hedwig's has another association. It's also the name of a 13th-century saint who lived in and around Germany. Hedwig was born to a duke and duchess and, at the age of 12, was married to King Henry I of Silesia. With her husband, she founded several important monasteries in Germany, as well as the region's first nunnery. She was also well known for working with leper women at a time when they were outcasts, for helping the poor and for giving away much of her family's fortune. After her husband was captured by a neighbouring prince over land that now lies in Poland, she rode for miles to secure his release. Although she had seven children, only one – an abbess called Gertrude – survived her. She died in 1243 and was made a saint just 24 years later.

— SECRET LIVES —

As the publication date for *Harry Potter And The Goblet Of Fire* approached, the ensuing media frenzy threatened to scale new heights. Hoping to surprise younger fans who might otherwise have been ambushed by the press, the book's publishers, Bloomsbury, and JK Rowling agreed to give the media the silent treatment, trusting it to lower the tempo of publicity. Consequently, the book's appearance and title were wrapped in secrecy. Only four people at Bloomsbury were allowed to read the book prior to its release. The manuscript was kept under the tightest security in a bank vault and its printers signed confidentiality pledges. Even so, the title was withheld from the proofs until the last possible minute.

Alas, the plan backfired as reporters, starved of information, went berserk in their quest for Potter news and gave more column inches to the forthcoming publication than ever before, broadcasting every meagre detail that came their way. Finally, the name of the new book leaked out via the internet before it was supposed to, apparently from an American source.

However, JK Rowling and the publishing staff she worked with had the last laugh. The launch of the book was followed by a tour on the *Hogwarts Express*, a specially hired steam train that transported Rowling across Britain, enabling her to meet as many fans as possible. What reporters didn't know was that her daughter, Jessica – always fiercely protected from public exposure by Rowling – was in the carriage, too. Everyone in the know agreed in advance to call the child Kate in order to maintain her privacy, although there were several slips of the tongue, not least from Rowling herself. Even so, none of the news-hungry press-hounds realised the identity of the important young passenger.

— THE SAME BUT DIFFERENT —

Only the most ardent Harry Potter fan will know that the American version of the book *Harry Potter And The Philosopher's Stone* (which is, of course, titled *Harry Potter And The Sorceror's Stone* in the US) has a character represented in greater detail than in its British counterpart. He is Dean Thomas, a black Londoner with a Muggle mother, who appears fleetingly in *Philosopher's Stone* but at greater length in *Sorcerer's Stone* in the chapter titled 'The Sorting Hat'.

Thomas was initially scheduled to appear in the British book, too, but he was cut out by an editor who felt that the chapter in which he appeared was too long. When the film was being made, JK Rowling took the opportunity to slot him back in so that British audiences could make his acquaintance.

It turns out that JK once had big plans in future books for Dean, whose father was killed by Death Eaters after refusing to join their number. However, his character was later cut a second time, this time by JK herself, who felt that his role wasn't compelling enough to warrant his survival. Still, she kept all her notes on him and has published them on her website.

— WHO IS ST MUNGO? —

The wizarding hospital in London is named for St Mungo, whose life straddled the sixth and seventh centuries and is still shrouded in mystery. Also known as Kentigern, it is thought that he was tutored by St Serf and eventually became the bishop of the small town that grew into Glasgow.

One tale remains strongly associated with him, although of course there's no proof it ever happened. Apparently, a local queen struck up a relationship with a soldier and sealed it with the gift of a ring that had previously been given to her by her husband, the king. Aware of the affair, the king removed the ring from the soldier's finger as he slept and tossed it into the River Clyde. The queen, unable to produce the ring on the command of her husband, was duly locked up and placed under threat of execution. She sent word to Bishop Mungo, who in turn had someone fish a salmon from the Clyde. In its gut – you guessed it – was the ring, which was restored to the queen, to her husband's mystification. She was freed but pledged never to make the same mistake again. It's for this reason that a salmon with a ring in its mouth is depicted on the Glaswegian coat of arms. This story is just one of a clutch of tales describing miracles attributed to St Mungo, who has since lent his name to a large London organisation for the homeless.

— SCHOOL REPORT —

After JK Rowling became internationally famous the press were hungry for details of her past life, especially her schooldays. In June 2000 Wyedean School in Chepstow offered a report on the school life of its most illustrious pupil, who joined its ranks of pupils in 1976. Her sister, Diane, also attended Wyedean, and their mother worked in the science department.

The report ran, 'Joanne proved to be a capable, academic student who always showed potential in all that she turned her hand to. After success in the pre-16 examinations, she elected to stay on in the school's sixth form, where she studied Modern Languages and English Literature at "A" level. Staff recall that, at this time, she had a preference for Modern Languages, and this was reflected in her choice of Classics and French when she left school and went on to Exeter University in 1983.

'Joanne was a popular and respected student who was liked by staff and other students, so much so that she was elected Head Girl and represented the school at a variety of functions.'

Stories penned by Rowling are now borrowed frequently from the school's library, whose staff and students, past and present, are among her greatest fans.

However, there's no mention from the school about the possible identity of the teacher upon whom Professor Snape is fashioned, whom Rowling has declined to name.

— WHAT NEXT? —

We're all waiting in anticipation for the next and, sadly, final instalment in the Harry Potter saga. JK Rowling had begun writing it by the time *Harry Potter And The Half-Blood Prince* was launched, but there's no completion or publication date in sight at the moment. Two years seems a likely estimate, as that's roughly how long it took to complete its predecessor. If that's the case, then two significantly neat dates come to mind. If the publication date was 7 July, the seventh book would be released on the seventh day of the seventh month of the seventh year of the new millennium. Alternatively, a June release in the same year could mark the tenth anniversary of the publication of Harry Potter's first adventure.

Whatever date is chosen, JK Rowling has uncharacteristically left us an indication of what lies ahead. In a recent interview published in *Time* magazine, she said, 'It will be a very different kind of book because I kind of cue up the shot at the end of six, and you're left with a very clear idea of what Harry's going to do next. And it will be exciting!'

Perhaps sufficient clues have already been laid. One long look in the pensieve might help fans figure out what lies ahead for Harry, Ron and Hermione. (If you're short on a rune-covered stone basin, use this book instead.) As

— WHAT NEXT? (CONT'D) —

Dumbedlore explained, with the overview it offers, it is quite the best method of spotting patterns and plotting important goings-on. And, after all, if it's good enough for Dumbledore...

APPENDIX

— CAST OF CHARACTERS —

Hannah Abbot – In the same year as Harry. Put into Hufflepuff by the Sorting Hat, she was one of Dumbledore's Army, but she's mostly remembered for turning a ferret into a flock of flamingos during her Charms practical exam.

Euan Abercrombie – A young Gryffindor.

Stuart Ackerly – Put into Ravenclaw by the Sorting Hat in *Harry Potter And The Goblet Of Fire*.

Agrippa – Knight, doctor, philosopher and ambassador, Cornelius Agrippa (1486–c1535) is best remembered for a respected tome on occultism. He appears on a Famous Witches and Wizards card.

Archie – The wizard in woman's clothing who tries to disguise himself as a Muggle during the Quidditch World Cup without realising that the flowery clothing he's chosen is inappropriate. He keeps it on, however, insisting that he 'enjoys some fresh air round his privates'.

Avery – Works as a Death Eater for Lord Voldemort and is sometimes punished by him for bungling.

Malcolm Baddock – Put into Slytherin by the Sorting Hat in *Harry Potter And The Goblet Of Fire*.

Ludo Bagman – Once one of the greatest Quidditch player of his time and now the head of a ministerial department, his work ethic coloured by a huge gambling addiction.

Otto Bagman – Ludo's brother, who had a little problem with the Ministry of Magic about a lawnmower with unnatural powers. Luckily for him, Arthur Weasley helped him out of trouble.

Millicent Bagnold – The Minister for Magic before Cornelius Fudge took over.

Bathilda Bagshot – Author of *A History Of Magic*.

Ali Bashir – Tried to introduce flying carpets into Britain. However, Arthur Weasley was having none of it, insisting that they were properly defined as a Muggle artefact.

Hetty Bayliss – One of the Muggles who saw Harry and Ron flying a car to Hogwarts.

Marcus Belby – Ravenclaw student with illustrious relations.

Katie Bell – Plays chaser on the Gryffindor Quidditch team. Also a member of Dumbledore's Army.

Amy Benson – Young victim of Voldemort's evil ways.

Professor Binns – History of Magic teacher and the only ghost on the Hogwarts staff.

Dennis Bishop – Another child bullied by the evil Lord Voldemort.

Alphard Black – Uncle and benefactor to Sirius.

Andromeda Black – Mother of Nymphadora Tonks and Sirius's favourite cousin.

Aunt Elladora Black – Started the tradition of beheading house elves when they were too weak or old to do any more work. Nice.

Regulus Black – Later brother of Sirius, murdered by Death Eaters after resigning from their number.

Sirius Black – Deemed one of the cleverest students during his time at Hogwarts by Professor McGonagall and Cornelius Fudge. He and his pal James Potter knew all the secret passages around Hogwarts' grounds, using them to great effect with their friend Lupin. His return to Hogwarts, however, was less than glorious. Sirius is the proper astronomical name for the Dog Star, the name of which derives from Greek mythology, where Sirius was the pet dog of the god Orion. In folklore, a black dog is often seen as a bad omen.

Miles Bletchey – Keeper on the Slytherin Quidditch team.

Stubby Boardman – Lead singer of The Hobgoblins.

Libatius Borage – Author of *Advanced Potion-Making*.

Broderick Bode – Ill-fated Ministry of Magic employee.

Amelia Susan Bones – Head of the Department of Magical Law Enforcement at the Ministry of Magic and the judge at Harry's hearing in *Harry Potter And The Order Of The Phoenix*.

Susan Bones – A niece of Amelia Susan Bones. Susan is in the same year as Harry, in Hufflepuff house, and was part of Dumbledore's Army.

Edgar Bones – A member of the original Order of the Phoenix. Edgar was killed, along with his family, by Lord Voldemort's followers. He is the brother of Amelia Bones.

Terry Boot – In the same year as Harry, Terry was put into Ravenclaw by the Sorting Hat and became a member of Dumbledore's Army.

Borgin – Proprietor of Borgin & Burkes, that dodgy emporium of all things evil.

Eleanor Branstone – Put into Hufflepuff by the Sorting Hat in *Harry Potter And The Goblet Of Fire*.

Mandy Bronkhurst – In the same year as Harry. Mandy was put into Ravenclaw by the Sorting Hat, after which she's not been mentioned.

Rupert 'Axebanger' Brookstanton – Well-known wizard from the past.

Lavender Brown – Lavender is typically girly, always giggling, but is good at heart. She went to the Yule Ball with Dean Thomas and is also a member of Dumbledore's Army.

Rosalind Antigone Bungs – Famous in the wizarding world but not linked to the present Hogwarts cast.

Caractacus Burke – One of the founders of Borgin & Burkes.

Frank Bryce – Wrongly accused by the habitants of Little Hangleton of killing the Riddles, Muggle Bryce came to momentary prominence after overhearing a conservation between Lord Voldemort and Peter Pettigrew.

Millicent Bulstrode – In the same year as Harry, Bulstrode is a bully. She has great fun with Neville when Hermione rejects his offer of a date. She went to the Yule Ball with Draco Malfoy.

Eddie Carmichael – Ravenclaw sixth-former who sells Ron and Harry Baruffio's Brain Elixir before their OWL exams.

Owen Cauldwell – Put into Hufflepuff by the Sorting Hat in *Harry Potter And The Goblet Of Fire*.

Cho Chang – Seeker on the Ravenclaw Quidditch team. Harry had a wild crush on her, but an attractive girl like Cho is never short of admirers.

Circe – In Greek mythology, Circe was the daughter of the sun who had the happy ability to turn men into animals with a swish of her wand. She is renowned for her knowledge of magic and poisons and appears on Famous Witches and Wizards cards.

Penelope Clearwater – Penelope went out with Percy for a while. Heaven knows what she was thinking.

Mrs Cole – Muggle orphanage matron.

Connolly – Beater on the Irish Quidditch team.

Ritchie Coote – Recently appointed Gryffindor beater.

Michael Corner – In the same year as Harry, in Ravenclaw, and a member of Dumbledore's Army.

Crabbe Sr – Father of Vincent Crabbe and part of Lord Voldemort's set-up, although he isn't terribly important.

Crabbe Jr – Dull-witted henchman of Draco Malfoy.

Colin Creevey – Colin is obsessed with Harry and always pesters him for photos as, curiously, his Muggle camera works perfectly at Hogwarts. However, Colin also has a big heart and will stick up for anybody as long as they're worth it.

Dennis Creevey – On his first day at school, Dennis fell into a lake containing a giant squid, yet on his emergence anyone would have thought he'd just come back from a fair. That's how excitable the Creeveys are.

Croaker – Works in the Department of Mysteries at the Ministry of Magic.

Doris Crockford – One of the locals at the Leaky Cauldron.

Bartemius Crouch Sr – Referred to as 'Barty' (to his great annoyance) by Ludo Bagman, Crouch Sr was dedicated to his profession and neglected his only son. Ambitious fathers, please note that he did so at his peril.

Bartemius Crouch Jr – A very promising prospect when he was young, but he later turned bad. Really bad.

Hector Dagworth-Granger – Founder of the Most Extraordinary Society of Potioneers.

Uncle Damocles – Relation of Marcus Belby much admired by Horace Slughorn for receiving an Order of Merlin, a wizarding equivalent to the Order of the British Empire, such as that awarded to JK Rowling.

Roger Davies – Ravenclaw Quidditch captain and chaser who went with Fleur Delacour to the Yule Ball in *Harry Potter And The Goblet Of Fire.*

Dawlish – Works for the Ministry of Magic.

Caradoc Dearbon – A member of the original Order of the Phoenix. His body vanished but he was certainly killed by Lord Voldemort's followers.

Fleur Delacour – A beautiful half-Veela girl who represented Beauxbatons in the Triwizard Tournament.

Gabrielle Delacour – Much-loved sister to Fleur.

Dilys Derwant – Worked in St Mungo's as a healer from 1722–41 and then became headmistress of Hogwarts from 1741–68. There is a painting of her in St Mungo's.

Dedalus Diggle – A cheerful soul who was probably the first wizard to shake Harry's hand. He practically lives at the Leaky Cauldron, where he chats with his mates and has the occasional drink, and is by all accounts very good company.

Amos Diggory – A generous man overtly proud of his son, Cedric.

Cedric Diggory – Kind and modest, Cedric is the noblest guy you could ever hope to meet.

Armando Dippet – Previously a Hogwarts headmaster.

Harold Dingle – A Hogwarts student, entrepreneur and scallywag who tried to sell crushed Doxy droppings as memory-enhancing dragon's claw during exams.

Emma Dobbs – A Hogwarts pupil.

Elphias Doge – A member of the original Order of the Phoenix.

Antonin Dolohov – Convicted Death Eater and an Azkaban escapee.

Mary Dorkins – A Muggle newsreader who reports on a spectacular water-skiing budgie.

Aberforth Dumbledore – Professor Dumbledore's brother, yet the complete opposite in character. He is unable to read and often gets into a lot of needless trouble with the Ministry of Magic (although perhaps that's not so difficult). He was also a member of the original Order of the Phoenix.

Albus Percival Wulfric Brian Dumbledore – It's said that Dumbledore is the only wizard that Lord Voldemort fears. Wise, powerful and humorous, he is the one person to whom everybody turns if they're in trouble. Indeed, Cornelius Fudge, in his early years of being Minister for Magic, came to Dumbledore frequently for advice. Headmaster of Hogwarts, member of the International Confederation of Wizards and Chief Warlock of the Wizengamot, he was an active member of the magical community. While he lost that status for a short period, he was soon reinstated after proving to everyone that the magical community needs him. The name Albus is actually the Latin word for 'white' but probably alludes to 'Albion' (a Roman term for 'Britain', possibly Celtic in origin), while Dumbledore is an Olde English word for bumblebee.

Dudley Dursley – Fat, stupid and a bully, Dudley is definitely the most dislikeable person in the Dursley family – and that's saying something. Terrifying all the children who are smaller than him, Dudley is now also a boxing champion, which makes him even more formidable than ever. Dennis, Malcom and Gordon are part of Dudley's gang.

Marge Dursley – Put Marge next to her brother, Vernon Dursley, and you'd be hard-pressed to tell them apart. Fat-necked, fat-bodied, fat-legged and fat-footed, Marge also has a moustache. She is obsessed with her bulldogs and takes her favourite dog, Ripper, with her wherever she goes. Dudley is like Marge's piggy bank, except the money she puts in never comes back out again. She treats Harry as if he's a slug.

Petunia Dursley – Physically, Petunia is the opposite to her husband, Vernon, being short, skinny and with a long neck (which comes in useful for spying on her neighbours). She is the sister of Harry's dead mother. Bitter from all the attention Lily got from their parents, Petunia abandoned her family to lead a 'normal' life. Unfortunately for her, however, baby Harry turns up on her doorstep and a mysterious letter convinces her to keep him.

Vernon Dursley – So fat he has about eight chins, Vernon failed to stamp the magic out of Harry but still tries to make his life as miserable as possible. Indeed, he relishes the cruelty he inflicts on Harry while treating his own son like a king. Afraid of magic, Vernon Dursley wants to be as 'normal' as possible.

Marietta Edgecombe – Cho's giggling friend who betrayed her pals. She didn't realise that she would end up with 'SNEAK' printed across her face.

Mark Evans – A victim of bullying by Dudley and his gang when aged just ten.

Lily Evans – Skilled potions maker, popular ex-Hogwarts pupil and Harry's loving mum. (See also *Lily Potter*.)

Benjy Fenwick – A member of the original Order of the Phoenix who was killed by Lord Voldemort's followers.

Arabella Doreen Figg – Mrs Figg is better known as the mad lady who keeps a lot of cats, but in fact she is a squib (ie an offspring of magical parents but with no powers) sent by Dumbledore to look after Harry while he is at the Dursleys'. The Dursleys do not suspect that she has anything to do with magic, and while they go out and have fun, Mrs Figg is Harry's minder.

Argus Filch – Less intelligent than Snape but equally unsavoury, Argus's secret is that he, like Mrs Figg, is a squib. He is nevertheless the head caretaker for the school and has banned all fun outside class. In Greek mythology Argus was a giant with 100 eyes who nevertheless failed in his caretaking duties.

Seamus Finnigan – One of Harry's roommates, Seamus was brought up in Ireland with his mother. He is a great laugh but is sometimes prone to gossip.

Firenze – Divination teacher and centaur.

Nicolas Flamel – Discovered the Philosopher's Stone and lived to a ripe old age because of it. He was close friends with Albus Dumbledore. There was, indeed, a real-life person named Nicolas Flamel who lived in 14th-century France and who was devoted to discovering the Philosopher's Stone and gaining the secrets of eternal life. Although he claimed to have cracked the alchemy code, there's no evidence that his life was prolonged as a result.

Perenelle Flamel – Wife of Nicolas and equally long-lived.

Angus Fleet – One of the Muggles who saw Harry and Ron flying a Ford Anglia to Hogwarts.

Mundungus Fletcher – Works for the Order of the Phoenix but failed in his mission to make sure that Harry was safe from harm in Privet Drive. According to JK Rowling, his unusual Christian name is Olde English for 'tobacco'.

Justin Finch Fletchley – An upper-crust Hogwarts pupil who also had his name down for top public school Eton. Fletchley was caught up in some trouble in his second year at Hogwarts and was turned to stone. He is also a member of Dumbledore's Army.

Professor Flitwick – Diminutive Charms teacher and head of Ravenclaw house.

Florean Fortescue – Ice-cream parlour proprietor and possibly a relation of a former Hogwarts headmaster of the same surname.

Vicky Frobisher – In Harry's fifth year, Vicky had a trial for the Gryffindor Quidditch team but eventually decided that Charms Club came first.

Cornelius Fudge – Minister for Magic. On the face of it bubbly and jolly, Cornelius is in truth very insecure and knows that the only reason why Professor Dumbledore isn't in the hot seat is because he doesn't want the job. Fudge refused to listen to reason concerning Lord Voldemort and lost credibility because of it.

Marvolo Gaunt – Tramp-like descendant of Salazar Slytherin with a vicious temper and extraordinary arrogance.

Merope Gaunt – Lovelorn and ill-starred daughter of Marvolo Gaunt.

Morfin Gaunt – Unprepossessing, parseltongue-speaking brother to Merope.

Miranda Gawshawk – Author of the Standard Book Of Spells series of books.

Anthony Goldstein – In the same year as Harry and put into Ravenclaw by the Sorting Hat. He is also a member of Dumbledore's Army.

Goyle Sr – Like father, like son. Goyle Sr is a stupid oaf and a Lord Voldemort devotee.

Gregory Goyle – Bulky and bone-headed, Goyle is always around when Draco Malfoy is in danger.

Hermione Granger – A clever, well-read witch who is very close to Ron and Harry, and indeed Hermione's sharp wits often keep them out of trouble. Her academic prowess is often recognised, and in *Harry Potter And The Prisoner Of Azkaban* Professor McGonagall gives her a time turner to enable her to attend more lessons than anyone else. In the same story, Lupin acknowledges to her, 'You're the cleverest witch of your age I've ever met.' However, she rues the fact that her knowledge is hewn from books rather than natural talent. She also forms part of a possible love triangle with Ron and Victor Krum, as well as one with Harry and Ron. She is a founder member of Dumbledore's Army.

Grawp – Knockabout half-brother of Hagrid, the kind of relation the rest of the family keep in a cupboard.

Daphne Greengrass – In the same year as Harry.

Fenrir Greyback – Savage contaminator.

Grindelwald – A dark wizard defeated by Dumbledore in 1945, at the same time that the Allies triumphed over Hitler in the Muggle world.

Griphook – A grumpy goblin that works at the wizard bank Gringotts.

Professor Wilhelmina Grubbly-Plank – A stand-in for Hagrid in the Care of Magical Creatures class and an effective teacher.

Alberic Grunnion – Appears on Famous Witches and Wizards cards.

Godric Gryffindor – One of the four people founders of Hogwarts. The house named after him stands for bravery. The lion on the Hogwarts flag is his emblem.

Davey Gudgeon – A pupil at Hogwarts when James Potter was at school. Gudgeon nearly lost an eye when he was foolish enough to play with the Whomping Willow.

Gladys Gudgeon – A huge fan of Gilderoy Lockhart.

Rubeus Hagrid – A jolly, kind-hearted half-giant, Hagrid means well in every single objective he is set. However, every single objective he is set seems to entail a problem. Hagrid had a tough childhood, but Dumbledore showed faith in him and was rewarded with a committed worker. Hagrid is great company.

Warty Harris – Helps Mundungus Fletcher in his dodgy dealings.

Heingst – Appears on Famous Witches and Wizards cards. Also the name of a Saxon king.

Bertie Higgs – Longtime friend of Scrimgeour.

Terence Higgs – During Harry's first year, Higgs played seeker for Slytherin. He might want to forget about that year.

Madam Hooch – Teaches first-years flying at Hogwarts. She is a big Quidditch fan and a very solid referee in the school Quidditch matches.

Geoffrey Hooper – Known mainly for his whingeing, it wasn't surprising when Hooper didn't get on the Gryffindor Quidditch team

Malfalda Hopkirk – An employee of the Ministry of Magic who sends out warning letters to those who have broken the law.

Olive Hornby – Hornby used to tease Moaning Myrtle all the time and was haunted for the rest of her life after Myrtle died.

Helga Hufflepuff – One of the four founders of Hogwarts. Hufflepuff house stands for loyalty. Her emblem is the badger.

Inigo Imago – Author of *Dream Oracle*.

Ivanova – Chaser on the Bulgarian Quidditch team.

Arsenius Jigger – Author of *Magical Drafts And Potions*.

Heistia – Works for the current Order of the Phoenix.

Gwenog Jones – Former Hogwarts pupil and captain of the Holyhead Harpies Quidditch team.

Lee Jordan – Like his pals Fred and George Weasley, Lee loves to play pranks. He is the Quidditch commentator for inter-house fixtures, accomplished Niffler handler and a member of Dumbledore's Army.

Bertha Jorkins – Jorkins went on holiday to Albania and unwittingly wandered off with a stranger named Wormtail, inadvertently providing Lord Voldemort with vital information.

Igor Karkaroff – Head of Durmstrang School of Witchcraft and Wizardry who used to work for Lord Voldemort. He grassed up his Voldemort co-workers in order to escape Azkaban.

Kevin – Went to the Quidditch World Cup with his family.

Andrew Kirke – Replaced Fred or George in one of the beater positions in the Gryffindor Quidditch team.

Viktor Krum – Described by many as one of the best Quidditch seekers in modern history, Krum is also one of the youngest. He was the favourite pupil of Durmstrang School's headmaster, Igor Karkaroff, which put him under a lot of pressure to perform as school champion in the Triwizard Tournament.

Bellatrix Lestrange – Works as a Death Eater for Lord Voldemort. Lestrange was sent to Azkaban prison for torturing Frank and Alice Longbottom into insanity.

Rodolphus Lestrange – A Death Eater for Lord Voldemort and Bellatrix Lestrange's husband.

Rabastan Lestrange – Rodolphus Lestrange's brother and one of Lord Voldemort's Death Eaters.

Levski – Chaser on the Bulgarian Quidditch team.

Dai Llewellyn – Quidditch player nicknamed 'Dangerous' Dai, in whose memory a ward has been named in St Mungo's.

Gilderoy Lockhart – One of the national wizarding 'heroes' who would have it believed that he's gone on many dangerous treks while paying little heed to his own personal safety. In fact, his magical powers are somewhat lacklustre. Many teachers questioned Dumbledore's decision to let him teach at Hogwarts in Harry's second year, and it turned out that they were right to be concerned.

Algie Longbottom – When Neville Longbottom was younger, his family wasn't sure whether he was a Muggle or not. Great-uncle Algie thought it would be a good idea to see if he could force some magic out of him, so he kept on trying to catch Neville off-guard, decided on one occasion to push him off a pier to see if anything happened. Nothing did. So much for pier support (geddit?).

Alice Longbottom – Alice was very popular in the wizarding community, just like her husband, Frank. She was tortured for the information she held about the Ministry of Magic and now resides in St Mungo's.

Frank Longbottom – Like his wife a very popular figure in the wizarding community, Frank too was tortured by Voldemort's forces seeking information on the Ministry of Magic, but also like Alice he did not submit.

Mrs Longbottom – Frank Longbottom's mother and Neville's grandmother. Now confined to St Mungo's, she is very proud of her son.

Neville Longbottom – Neville is similar to Harry in more ways than one: he's loyal, brave and comes from a family devoted to suppressing the dark arts. Indeed, he and Harry are so similar that Lord Voldemort had to choose between Harry and Neville to be his equal, according to a prophecy. Neville also has the same enemies as Harry, receiving a pretty hard time at the hands of Malfoy, Crabbe and Goyle, although he has shown that he can defend himself against them. He is scared to death by Snape, however, as he demonstrated when he faced a boggart that took on the teacher's form when representing Neville's worst fear. He is often forgetful, but that's hardly surprising considering that he has such a lot on his mind.

Luna Lovegood – Something of a troubled child, Luna has difficulty making friends because of her offbeat outlook on life. Her mother died in an experiment that went wrong when Luna was only nine, though she and her father have since recovered from the blow.

Mr Lovegood – Widowed father of Luna and editor of *The Quibbler* magazine.

Remus Lupin – One of James Potter's best friends at school. He was attacked by a werewolf and so couldn't do as much as he would have liked to when he was at school in case he hurt one of his friends. However, his friends found out the truth and stuck by him. He is now a member of the Order of the Phoenix.

Aidan Lynch – Seeker on the Irish national Quidditch team.

Nathalie Macdonald – Macdonald was put into Gryffindor by the Sorting Hat in Harry's fourth year at Hogwarts.

Morag Macdougal – Hogwarts student in the same year as Harry.

Ernie Macmillan – In the same year as Harry, Ernie Macmillan is fairly pompous and a bit prone to gossip, but he means no harm. He is also part of Dumbledore's Army.

Walden Macnair – When he was caught in the Voldemort circle by the Ministry of Magic, Macnair managed to worm his way out of trouble by spinning a cock-and-bull story. He now works as an executioner for them.

Laura Madley – Put into Hufflepuff by the Sorting Hat in Harry's fourth year at Hogwarts.

Abraxas Malfoy – Draco's grandad, who died following a bout of dragon pox.

Draco Malfoy – Slick, sly and prejudiced, Malfoy is probably the most hateful boy in Hogwarts. His name is a French translation of 'bad faith', and he has long been earmarked to join Lord Voldemort.

Lucius Malfoy – Like father, like son. Lucius holds exactly the same views as his son on virtually everything. He is very snooty and spiteful, although bigwigs at the Ministry of Magic believed that he was, in fact, a generous benefactor. Hmm.

Narcissa Malfoy – Mrs Malfoy doesn't seem to care what her husband is up to, and she would give her son anything he wanted. Her name is the female form of Narcissus, who in Greek mythology fell in love with his own reflection and whose name has since been used as a by-word for vanity.

Madam Malkin – Owner of the shop Madam Malkin's Robes For All Occasions, where Harry first met Draco Malfoy.

Griselda Marchbanks – Resigned in protest from the Wizengamot because she felt that the 'minister was using the school as an outpost for Cornelius Fudge's office'. She is also an exam adjudicator.

Madam Marsh – A regular on the Knight Bus – unfortunately for her, as she suffers from motion sickness.

Olympe Maxime – Reluctant half-giant and head of Beauxbatons School of Witchcraft and Wizardry, Olympe is a powerful witch who has a tentative relationship with Hagrid.

Minerva McGonagall – Professor McGonagall is probably the strictest teacher at Hogwarts, but her gruff exterior hides the fact she's also the fairest and most caring. She's also a part-time cat. As head of Gryffindor, she is exceptionally dedicated to her house and very interested in how the Quidditch team are doing. She proved this by getting Harry the best broomstick of the day (the now-dated Nimbus 2000) and enabling Harry to be the first first-year to play Quidditch for his house for a whole century.

Jim McGuffin – A confused weatherman who expressed his bafflement when, 'instead of rain that I promised yesterday, there has been a downpour of shooting stars.' This phenomenon occurred, of course, when Harry Potter defeated Lord Voldemort for the first time.

Cormac McLaggen – Hogwarts student in Gryffindor.

Marlene McKinnon – A member of the original Order of the Phoenix, McKinnon was killed, along with her family, by Lord Voldemort's followers.

Dorcas Meadows – A member of the original Order of the Phoenix. Voldemort killed her himself.

Araminta Meliflua – A cousin of Sirius Black's mother who attempted to make Muggle-hunting legal. Lovely lady.

Merlin – A wizard of immense importance (see pages 28–9). He appears on Famous Witches and Wizards cards.

Galatea Merrythought – Longstanding Defence Against the Dark Arts teacher in Tom Riddle's era.

Eloise Midgeon – Known mainly for her blooming acne, Eloise is actually quite nice. However, she isn't the most intelligent girl in the school and once attempted to curse her spots away, with disastrous results.

Martin Miggs – The 'mad Muggle' and subject of a favourite wizard comic.

Sir Nicholas de Mimsy-Porpington – Otherwise known (to his displeasure) as Nearly Headless Nick, Sir Nicholas died at Hogwarts following the attentions of an incompetent axeman on 31 October 1492. Despite being a ghost, a basilisk paralysed him in Harry's second year at Hogwarts.

Cuthbert Mockridge – Head of the Goblin Liaison Office at the Ministry of Magic.

Montague – Marcus Flint's successor as captain of the Slytherin Quidditch team.

Alastor Moody – One of Dumbledore's closest friends and one of the best aurors in the business, not least because he is suspicious of everyone and everything.

Moran – Chaser on the Irish national Quidditch team.

Morgana – Merlin's adversary. Appears on Famous Witches and Wizards cards.

Hassan Mostafa – One-time chair of the International Association of Quidditch and the referee in charge of the World Cup final.

Mulciber – Worked as a Death Eater for Lord Voldemort.

Mullet – Chaser on the Irish national Quidditch team.

Eric Munch – A watchwizard for the Ministry of Magic.

Madam Z Nettes – Nettes was a squib who resorted to Kwikspell, a correspondence course in wand use.

Phineas Nigellus – Sirius Black's great-grandfather and the least popular of all the headmasters of Hogwarts. He has little time for his great-grandson, and yet they are somewhat alike.

Mrs Norris – The feline soulmate of Argus Filch. She follows him around everywhere and has a terrifically sensitive nose.

Theodore Nott – In the same year as Harry, Nott was put into Slytherin by the Sorting Hat. His father is a Death Eater.

Bob Ogden – Former head of the Department of Magical Law Enforcement Squad with questionable dress sense.

Tiberius Ogden – Resigned in protest from the Wizengamot because of Cornelius Fudge's behaviour.

Mr Ollivander – Runs the only wand business in town. He also remembers every single person who buys a wand from his shop and is a tad sinister in his behaviour.

Paracelsus – A 16th-century alchemist who rarely used his full name of Auroleus Phillipus Theophrastus Bombastus von Hohenheim. He appears on Famous Witches and Wizards cards, and there's also a bust of him at Hogwarts.

Pansy Parkinson – Enthusiastic Slytherin with her sights set on Draco Malfoy.

Padma Patil – In the same year as Harry. Padma was put into a different house from her twin sister, which is unusual in Hogwarts.

Parvati Patil – Unsurprisingly, Parvati is, like her twin sister, Padma, in the same year as Harry. She is best friends with Lavender Brown, went to the Yule Ball with Harry and is a member of Dumbledore's Army.

Jimmy Peakes – Gryffindor Quidditch team recruit.

Arnold Peasegood – An obliviator (ie a member of the Accidental Magic Reversal Squad).

Peter Pettigrew – All Pettigrew is concerned about is himself, and whoever is the big fish in his pond gets his support. This is why he was 'friends' with James Potter, Remus Lupin and Sirius Black. He is currently considering his options.

Madam Pince – A bossy librarian whose sole purpose in life is to make sure that there isn't one crumb of food in the library, ever. She and Argus Filch should get together sometime.

Sturgis Podmore – Podmore was caught in the act while trying to retrieve something for the Order of the Phoenix from inside the Ministry. He was sentenced six months in Azkaban.

Poliakoff – A student at Durmstrang School of Witchcraft and Wizardry.

Piers Polkiss – Dudley Dursley's closest friend. Piers follows Dudley around like a puppy dog and will help beat up anyone Dudley wants beaten up.

Madam Pomfrey – Being the Hogwarts nurse, Madam Pomfrey has probably seen Harry more than the Dursleys have.

Harry Potter – Harry is known to the wizarding community as 'the boy who lived' following an incident with Voldemort in which his parents were killed. He was condemned to stay with the Dursleys for the rest of his childhood, ignorant of his wizard heritage, until the fateful day that Rubeus Hagrid appeared and told him all he needed to know about Hogwarts. From that day forth, Harry has been counting the days every summer holiday until he can return to school, where he can be himself. Talented at Quidditch, he has quite an impressive CV, defeating Lord Voldemort on a handful of occasions and killing a basilisk along the way.

James Potter – In his time at Hogwarts, James, Sirius Black, Remus Lupin and Peter Pettigrew were the 'rebels' in his year, and probably throughout the school. He met his future wife, Lily, in Hogwarts, although at first things didn't work out; Lily thought he was a big-headed scumbag, James thought she was a fox and, let's face it, we know the story. After a while, however, Lily saw a lot more in James than first met the eye. Harry is recognised as James's son as they look alike. James's memory is respected throughout the wizarding world, except by a few, specifically Snape, who loathed James from the minute they met.

Lily Potter – Sacrificing her life for Harry – and, by extension, many others – Lily gave a powerful protection to her young son that has kept him alive against all odds. She showed initiative, bravery and brilliance beyond imagining. Harry has inherited her eyes.

Roddy Ponter – Had a bet with Ludo Bagman that Bulgaria would score first in the Quidditch World Cup final between Bulgaria and Ireland.

Ernie Prang – Drives the Knight Bus.

Fabian Prewett – A member of the original Order of the Phoenix, Prewett died a hero alongside his brother, Gideon.

Gideon Prewett – Like his brother, Fabian, Gideon was a member of the original Order of the Phoenix. It took five Death Eaters to kill them.

Eileen Prince – Unlikely mother of one nasty piece of work.

Apollyn Pringle – A former and caretaker at Hogwarts equally fierce as Filch, Pringle once caught a young Arthur Weasley out and about past bedtime. Weasley still bears the scars.

Graham Pritchard – Put into Slytherin by the Sorting Hat in the year of the Triwizard Tournament.

DJ Prod – A squib who resorted to Kwikspell.

Claudius Ptolemy – An astronomer and geographer in Roman times. He also appears on Famous Witches and Wizards cards.

Madam Puddifoot – Owns a small tea shop in Hogsmeade.

Doris Purkiss – Interviewed in *The Quibbler* concerning Sirius Black's whereabouts. If there was a competition in dottiness between Doris and Professor Trelawney, Purkiss would win, mainly because she thinks that Sirius Black is a successful singer playing for The Hobgoblins.

Augustus Pye – A trainee healer at St Mungo's.

Quigley – Beater on the Irish Quidditch team.

Orla Quirke – Put into Ravenclaw by the Sorting Hat in the year of the Triwizard Tournament.

Professor Quirrel – A stuttering, deceitful character who is unwittingly exploited by Lord Voldemort. He taught Defence Against the Dark Arts in Harry's first year at Hogwarts.

Urquhart Rackharrow – Invented the entrail-expelling curse.

Ragnok – Significant goblin.

Rowena Ravenclaw – One of the four founders of Hogwarts. Ravenclaw house stands for cleverness, its emblem being an eagle.

Tom Riddle (Lord Voldemort) – Tom Riddle had a tough childhood. His father left his mother when she was pregnant, then his mother tragically died while giving birth to him (although that doesn't mean he has to take it out on everybody else). He considers himself to be the greatest dark lord of all time. However, there is one whom he considers his equal: Harry Potter. He also fears Dumbledore (with good reason) and trusts only one thing: his faithful pet snake, Ngini.

Demelza Robins – Gryffindor Quidditch team hopeful.

Augustus/Algernon Rookwood – One of Lord Voldemort's Death Eaters who worked inside the Ministry of Magic, feeding vital information back to him.

Evan Rosier – Worked as a Death Eater for Lord Voldemort and was consequently killed.

Barry Ryan – Keeper for the Irish national Quidditch team.

Newt Scamander – Author of *Fantastic Beasts And Where To Find Them*.

Rufus Scrimgeour – Ambitious and successful Ministry man and a bureaucrat through to his bones.

Kingsley Shacklebolt – Works incognito for the Order of the Phoenix. Shacklebolt gathers information from the Ministry of Magic, and no one suspects him of working with Dumbledore.

Stan Shunpike – Does a number of numerous jobs, such as helping with the Knight Bus. Shunpike is next in line to be the youngest Minister for Magic (he wishes).

Professor Sinistra – Teaches Astronomy at Hogwarts.

Rita Skeeter – A strident journalist who ruins people's lives with her ill-advised and unproven words. She met her downfall in Hermione Granger. She is now in a position to be used against Lord Voldemort by spreading the news that he is back.

Wilbert Slinkhard – Author of *Defensive Magical Theory*.

Jack Sloper – Replaced Fred or George in one of the beater positions in the Gryffindor Quidditch team.

Horace Slughorn – Corpulent professor largely oblivious to the threat posed by Voldemort.

Salazar Slytherin – One of the four founders of Hogwarts. Slytherin house prizes cunning among its members, and its emblem on the Hogwarts flag is a serpent.

Veronica Smethley – Another huge fan of Gilderoy Lockhart's.

Hippocrates Smethwyck – A senior healer at St Mungo's. The Hippocratic oath taken by Muggle doctors is not named for him, however, but for the Greek doctor Hippocrates, born in about 460 BC.

Hepzibah Smith – A rich, vain and silly old witch.

Zacharias Smith – Smith is in the same year as Harry and was put into Hufflepuff by the Sorting Hat, later becoming a chaser in the house Quidditch team. He questioned the belief that Lord Voldemort had returned and was reluctant to join Dumbledore's Army.

Severus Snape – Physically unattractive and grossly unpleasant, Snape lost the title of most hated teacher at Hogwarts to Professor Umbridge. His life was saved by James Potter, which put him in debt to the Potter family. This was unfortunate for Snape, as he hates every single one of them.

Tobias Snape – Father of the slimy prof.

Alicia Spinnet – Chaser on the Gryffindor Quidditch team.

Phyllida Spore – Author of *One Thousand Magical Herbs And Fungi*.

Professor Sprout – Aptly named Herbology teacher and head of Hufflepuff.

Patricia Stimpson – Fainted due to nervousness over her OWL exams.

Miriam Strout – A healer at St Mungo's hospital.

Billy Stubbs – Scab-picking, rabbit-keeping Muggle orphan.

Grogan Stump – 19th-century Minister for Magic.

Emeric Switch – Author of *A Beginners' Guide To Transfiguration*.

Dean Thomas – In the same year as Harry and the same house and dormitory. He is probably the only football fan in the entire school and is a member of Dumbledore's Army.

Uncle Tiberius – Relative of Cormac McLaggen possibly named for the somewhat unsavoury second Roman emperor who died in AD 37 following a life of gluttony and debauchery.

Agatha Timms – Gambled with Ludo Bagman that a Quidditch World Cup match would go on for a week. Unfortunately, she lost half her winnings on her eel farm.

Professor Tofty – Examiner at the Ministry of Magic.

Nymphadora Tonks – Works for the Order of the Phoenix and is a metamorphagus. She is closely related to Sirius Black and prefers to be called simply 'Tonks'.

Ted Tonks – Muggle father of Nymphadora Tonks.

Kenneth Towler – Towler is in the same year as Fred and George Weasley. He had a breakdown during his OWL exams.

Travers – Worked as a Death Eater for Lord Voldemort.

Cassandra Trelawney – A well-respected seer and ancestor of Professor Trelawney.

Professor Trelawney – Sherry-swigging Divination teacher with unexpected hidden talents.

Quentin Trimble – Author of *The Dark Forces: A Guide To Self-Protection*.

Troy – Chaser on the Irish national Quidditch team.

Lisa Turpin – Turpin is in the same year as Harry and was put into Ravenclaw by the Sorting Hat.

Dolores Umbridge – One of the most hated teachers of all time. Many teachers give lines for detention, but she thinks it is humane to etch the words into her pupils' skin. She worked for the Ministry of Magic and succeeded in overthrowing Dumbledore in pursuit of complete control. However, she was in for an unexpectedly rough ride.

Cassandra Vablatski – Author of *Unfogging The Future*.

Emmeline Vance – A member of the original Order of the Phoenix.

Romilda Vane – Young Hogwarts pupil with a powerful crush on Harry.

Professor Vindictus Viridion – Author of *Curses And Counter-curses*.

Volkov – Beater on the Bulgarian national Quidditch team.

Vulchanov – Beater on the Bulgarian national Quidditch team.

Adalbert Waffling – Author of *Magical Theory*.

Celestina Warbeck – A successful witch singer.

Warrington – Currently a chaser on the Slytherin Quidditch team.

Arthur Weasley – Ministry employee, Order of the Phoenix member and head of the Weasley family. He is obsessed with Muggles and is fascinated by the electrical items they create.

Bill Weasley – Ron's oldest brother. He works in a branch of Gringotts Bank somewhere in South Africa.

Charlie Weasley – Described as one of the best Quidditch players Hogwarts has ever had, Charlie is the second oldest son in the Weasley family. He works as a dragon tamer for the Ministry of Magic.

Ginny Weasley – In her first year, Ginny was immediately attracted to Harry and was very shy. She then came to feel a lot more comfortable around him and became a lot more outgoing, just like her brothers. Ginny is a clever witch who found herself in a very unpleasant situation in Harry's second year.

Fred and George Weasley – These two are exactly the same in every way, shape and form. They were described by Hagrid as the only two mischief-makers who could come close to touching Sirius Black and James Potter. However, they are very noble towards their family and would do anything to protect them.

Molly Weasley – Caring, loving and sometimes a little over-protective, Molly has found herself in the role of a part-time parent to Harry. She took an immediate shine to him and has helped him through some very difficult situations during his time at Hogwarts. Harry has repaid her by saving her daughter's life in his second year.

Percy Weasley – Percy used to be the Weasley who achieved all the top grades, earning him the title 'Perfect Percy'. This attitude changed when he became obsessed with the Ministry of Magic, at the expense of his family.

Ron Weasley – Ron is perhaps the most genuine and generally loyal person at Hogwarts. As soon as Harry met him, a close bond was formed between them that has since grown and flourished. Ron and Harry have only ever had one argument, which is remarkable considering that they spend so much time around one other. Ron is rather sensitive about his family's lack of money, although, having met Harry, he perhaps now understands better the value of a happy, loving family. He is put in the shade academically by Hermione and magically by Harry. Nevertheless, he doesn't feel diminished by this and inevitably proves his worth as a stout and courageous friend.

Eric Whalley – Muggle orphan smothered with oozing chicken pox.

Kennilworthy Whisp – Quidditch expert, Wigtown Wanderers fan and author of *Quidditch Through The Ages*.

Kevin Whitby – Whitby was put into Hufflepuff by the Sorting Hat in the year of the Triwizard Tournament

Willy Wildershins – Got involved with some regurgitating toilets, for which he was blackmailed by the Ministry of Magic to tell them about the meeting Harry held in order to form a Defence Against the Dark Arts group, which was later made illegal in an attempt to get Harry expelled.

Gilbert Wimple – Member of the Committee of Experimental Charms.

Blaise Zabini – Zabini is in the same year as Harry and was put into Slytherin by the Sorting Hat.

Ladislaw Zamojski – Known as the best chaser on the Polish national Quidditch team.

Rose Zeller – Joined Hogwarts in *Harry Potter And The Order Of The Phoenix* and was put into Hufflepuff by the Sorting Hat.

Zograf – Keeper on the Bulgarian national Quidditch team.

— GLOSSARY OF TERMS —

Alchemy – A blend of chemistry and magic that was especially popular in the Middle Ages, when men used it in an attempt to find (a) immortality and (b) the ability to transform base metals into gold.

Animagus – Witch or wizard with the ability to transform into an animal. Animaguses are rare and all are supposed to be registered with the Ministry of Magic. One particularly famous animagus, according to author TH White, was the magician Merlin. The word *magus* is Latin for 'wizard'.

Auror – Wizard working exclusively to defeat those involved in the dark arts. The name is probably derived from the word 'aura', an envelope of mystical energy that's said to be possessed by all creatures and objects.

Avada Kedavra – This spell, its name deriving from ancient Aramaic (the language spoken by Jesus and his contemporaries) and translating to 'vanish like this word', was traditionally used as a defence against plagues. It is almost certainly the historical origin of the commonly used 'magic' word 'abracadabra'. However, there's nothing rabbit-out-of-the-hat-like about the words *avada kedavra* in Harry's wizarding world. This is a killing curse – the one used to murder Harry's parents, in fact – against which there is no counter-curse. Although a bolt of green light issues from the spellcaster when the curse is uttered, the victims are left without a mark. Along with the Imperius and Cruciatus curses, the Avada Kedavra curse is classed as an Unforgivable Curse and use of it will bring about a life sentence for its user inside Azkaban.

Beauxbatons – A wizarding school in France, the 'beautiful sticks' of its name presumably applying to wands.

Dark Mark – The skull-and-serpent sign etched on the skin of Voldemort's followers. The idea is presumably inspired by the Devil's mark, a medieval interpretation of bodily blemishes, including moles and nipples, that supposedly indicated that a person was a witch.

Durmstrang – A wizarding college whose pupils wear blood-red cloaks and specialise in the dark arts. Located in the colder reaches of northern Europe, the school's name is derived by the German words for 'storm' and 'stress' and is a term that also applies to the cultural arts associated with nationalism in Germany. This is entirely appropriate as, like German nationalists in the first half of the 20th century, Durmstrang is proud of having a pure pupil pedigree and is opposed to those who are ethnically different.

Elixir of Life – A potion mixed by an alchemist that brings about everlasting life.

Floo Powder – A compound used by wizards for transportation and communication, usually operating between fireplaces.

Galleon – Unit of wizarding money.

Goblet of Fire – Rough wooden cup 'full to the brim' with flames that imbues those who drink from it with great wisdom. It is from this vessel that the names of the school champions are drawn for the Triwizard Tournament. It's similar in many respects to the Holy Grail, the cup used by Jesus at the Last Supper and sought ever since for its mystical properties.

Hand of Glory – An item that fascinated Draco Malfoy in Knockturn Alley. A hand of glory is actually the severed limb of a hanged man. Hands of glory were once reputed to have magical powers and were highly sought after during the 18th and 19th centuries, when hanging was the usual punishment for relatively insignificant crimes.

Horcrux – Dark arts device used to secretly store sections of the soul. It can take any form, but the soul-splitting thing must follow a vile murder.

Knockturn Alley – Less reputable shopping centre for wizards.

Knut – The least valuable unit of wizarding money.

Invisibility Cloak – As its name implies, this is a cloak that makes everything beneath it vanish from sight.

Magizoology – The study of magical or mythical creatures.

Mermish – The language of the Merpeople.

Metamorphmagus – A witch or wizard able to transform their appearance at a whim. Nymphadora Tonks is a metamorphagus.

Mudblood – Derisory term for a wizard with Muggle parentage.

Muggle – Wizarding term for a non-magical human.

NEWTs – Nastily Exhausting Wizarding Tests, taken by Hogwarts pupils in their seventh year. As with OWLs, the grades are as follows: O for 'Outstanding', E for 'Exceeds Expectations' and A for 'Acceptable', while failing grades are P for 'Poor', D for 'Dreadful' and T for 'Troll'.

OWLS – Ordinary Wizarding Level qualifications.

Parseltongue – The language of snakes, known by both Harry and Voldemort.

Pensieve – Receptacle for thoughts.

Sickle – Unit of wizarding money.

Sorting Hat – Rhyming and mind-reading piece of ancient headgear used annually for matching new Hogwarts pupils with their most appropriate house.

Squib – Someone born of magician stock but with no magic powers.

Veela – Beguiling witch from Bulgaria.

— ACTING UP —

The ultimate who's who of Harry Potter films.

ROBBIE COLTRANE (RUBEUS HAGRID)

OTHER CREDITS: *Van Helsing* (2004), *The World Is Not Enough* (1999), *Cracker* (UK TV series).

GUESS WHAT? He loves cars, jazz, gambling, drinking – and his son was an extra in the Harry Potter movies. He gets on famously with the young actors on the Harry Potter set, who like to play tricks on him. Consequently, he also enjoys getting his revenge.

QUOTABLE QUOTE: 'If the camera's on them and you stick your finger up your nose, they're gone.'

KENNETH BRANAGH (PROFESSOR GILDEROY LOCKHART)

OTHER CREDITS: *Shackleton* (2002), *Rabbit Proof Fence* (2002), *Hamlet* (1996).

GUESS WHAT? Known for his links to Shakespeare's work, Branagh was one of the directors considered for *Harry Potter And The Prisoner Of Azkaban* and spent his early years in Belfast when the city was in strife.

QUOTABLE QUOTE: 'There was a sword fight and the night before I'd had a few drinks. I was the Heineken Hamlet, the hungover Hamlet. The sword fell apart in my hand and I started to laugh. I was crying but they weren't the right tears [for the part].'

GARY OLDMAN (SIRIUS BLACK)

OTHER CREDITS: *Dead Fish* (2004), *JFK* (1991), *Sid And Nancy* (1986).

GUESS WHAT? A welder's son, Oldman was once married to Uma Thurman. He often plays sinister or downright psychotic characters.

QUOTABLE QUOTES: 'I would imagine that, when it comes to romantic comedies, my name would be pretty low down on the list.'

RICHARD HARRIS (PROFESSOR ALBUS DUMBLEDORE)

OTHER CREDITS: *Gladiator* (2002), *Camelot* (1967), *The Snow Goose* (1971).

GUESS WHAT? Born and brought up in Ireland, where he was a keen rugby player, Harris got to Number Two in the 1968 Top 40 with the single 'MacArthur Park'. He took on the role of Dumbledore only after his 11-year-old granddaughter said she would never speak to him again if he didn't.

QUOTABLE QUOTES: 'Don't you dare recast me!' to director Chris Columbus from his hospital bed shortly before his death.

JOHN CLEESE (NEARLY HEADLESS NICK)

OTHER CREDITS: *Die Another Day* (2002), *Monty Python And The Holy Grail* (1975), *Fawlty Towers* (UK TV series).

GUESS WHAT? John was 6ft tall at 12 years old, when he was a talented cricketer. He created Basil Fawlty after staying in a hotel in Torbay owned by a man just like him!

QUOTABLE QUOTES: 'That, sir, is an ex-parrot.'

CHRISTIAN COULSON (TOM RIDDLE)

OTHER CREDITS: *The Hours* (2002), *The Forsythe Saga* (UK TV mini-series).

GUESS WHAT? Although both are big Shakespeare fans, Coulson did not meet co-star Kenneth Branagh until the film premiere of *Harry Potter And The Chamber Of Secrets*. Coulson also starred in the 2001 UK TV series *Weirdsister College*. Spooky!

QUOTABLE QUOTES: 'I can't watch stuff I'm in without cringing all the way through.'

WARWICK DAVIES (PROFESSOR FLITWICK AND A GOBLIN BANK TELLER)

OTHER CREDITS: *Willow* (1988), *Star Wars: Episode VI – Return Of The Jedi* (1983)

GUESS WHAT? Although he has now reached 3ft 6ins in height, Davies measured just 2ft 11in when he was in *Return Of The Jedi*.

QUOTABLE QUOTES: He now runs Willow Personal Management, which he describes as 'the biggest agency for short actors in the world'.

MICHAEL GAMBON (PROFESSOR ALBUS DUMBLEDORE)

Other films credits: *Ali G Indahouse* (2002), *The Wind In The Willows* (1995), *The Cook, The Thief, His Wife And Her Lover* (1989)

GUESS WHAT? He was once considered for the role of James Bond after actor George Lazenby bombed, but he was turned down because he wasn't famous enough. He hated school, having been beaten by the masters at his, and he loves antique weaponry.

QUOTABLE QUOTE: 'Theatre actors are just tolerated. You have to be a movie star to be a celebrity.'

RICHARD GRIFFITHS (UNCLE VERNON DURSLEY)

OTHER CREDITS: *Chariots Of Fire* (1981), *Gandhi* (1982), *Withnail And I* (1987)

GUESS WHAT? His parents were both deaf-mutes, so Griffiths has full working knowledge of sign language. He was devastated that all scenes involving the Dursleys were being cut out of *Harry Potter And The Goblet of Fire* because the movie would otherwise be too long.

QUOTABLE QUOTES: 'I said to JK Rowling, "Couldn't the Dursleys turn up to an open day at Harry's school or something?" But she said, "I don't think so."'

IAN HART (PROFESSOR QUIRREL)
OTHER CREDITS: *Strictly Sinatra* (2001), *Longitude* (TV movie, 2000), *Finding Neverland* (2004).

GUESS WHAT? Liverpudlian Ian has twice played assassinated Beatles hero John Lennon, and he's also been Dr John Watson twice in Sherlock Holmes thrillers.

QUOTABLE QUOTES: 'I hate me. I always see the mistakes I made. Just because someone else didn't notice it, it doesn't mean that it isn't there.'

SHIRLEY HENDERSON (MOANING MYRTLE)
OTHER CREDITS: *Trainspotting* (1996), *Bridget Jones's Diary* (2001), *Bridget Jones: The Edge Of Reason* (2004).

GUESS WHAT? As a youngster, Shirley appeared on the UK TV talent show *Opportunity Knocks* and sang between bouts at a local boxing ring. Once, when she was filming in Russia, she saw a ghost!

QUOTABLE QUOTES: 'I'd describe [Myrtle's] voice as wounded. I did a lot of crying during the scenes, and that aided that kind of gurgly quality I was trying to produce, as if she was choking on water all the time.'

JOHN HURT (MR OLLIVANDER)
OTHER CREDITS: *Captain Corelli's Mandolin* (2001), *The Elephant Man* (1980), *Alien* (1979).

GUESS WHAT? John, the son of a clergyman, was in make-up for seven hours every day that he played John Merrick in *The Elephant Man*.

QUOTABLE QUOTES: 'I have had some mischievous moments where I should have behaved more responsibly.'

JASON ISAACS (LUCIUS MALFOY)
OTHER CREDITS: *Dragonheart* (1996), *Black Hawk Down* (2001), *Resident Evil* (2002), *Peter Pan* (2003).

GUESS WHAT? The third of four sons, Jason is a keen tennis player. He's also well known for being in the long-running US TV series *The West Wing*.

QUOTABLE QUOTES: 'I could release myself into acting in a way that I was not released socially.'

TOBY JONES (VOICE OF DOBBY, THE HOUSE ELF)
OTHER CREDITS: *Ladies In Lavender* (2004), *Finding Neverland* (2004), *Midsomer Murders* (UK TV series).

GUESS WHAT? A talented impressionist, Jones won an award for his part in the West End hit *The Play What I Wrote*, a tribute to British comedians Morecambe and Wise. When Sir Bob Geldof was a special guest in the show, Jones called him Mr Dandruff, Gandalf and Bob Monkhouse.

QUOTABLE QUOTES: 'I'm desperate to play James Bond.'

MIRIAM MARGOYLES (PROFESSOR SPROUT)

OTHER CREDITS: *Cats And Dogs* (2001), *Mulan* (1998), *Babe* (1995).

GUESS WHAT? Although she was educated at Cambridge University, Miriam now lives in Sydney, Australia.

QUOTABLE QUOTES: 'I have been fat all my life and I expect to die fat, but I'm not fat inside. I'm a little darting thing with quick movements to match my quick mind, and when I realised I was fat – which was probably when I was 11 – I decided to use it to my advantage.'

ALAN RICKMAN (PROFESSOR SEVERUS SNAPE)

OTHER CREDITS: *Robin Hood: Prince Of Thieves* (1991), *Truly, Madly, Deeply* (1991), *Die Hard* (1988)

GUESS WHAT? Alan was once a graphic designer, he loves rollercoaster rides and at the age of seven he took the lead role in a school play titled *King Grizzly Beard*.

QUOTABLE QUOTE: 'Give me a window and I'll stare out of it.'

FIONA SHAW (AUNT PETUNIA DURSLEY)

OTHER CREDITS: *Anna Karenina* (1997), *Jane Eyre* (1996), *3 Men And A Little Lady* (1990)

GUESS WHAT? Born in County Cork, Eire, Fiona became famous for her new-gender agenda by taking the lead role in Shakespeare's *Richard II*.

QUOTABLE QUOTES: 'A lot of Irish people perform. They perform in drawing rooms. They sing songs and they play piano.'

MAGGIE SMITH (PROFESSOR MINERVA McGONAGALL)

Other credits: *The Prime Of Miss Jean Brodie* (1969), *A Private Function* (1984), *David Copperfield* (UK TV film, 1999).

GUESS WHAT? Maggie was made a Dame Commander of the Most Excellent Order of the British Empire in 1990, and her middle name is Natalie.

QUOTABLE QUOTE: 'One went to school, one wanted to act and one's still acting.'

VERNE TROYER (GRIPHOOK THE GOBLIN)

OTHER CREDITS: *Austin Powers In Goldmember* (2002), *How The Grinch Stole Christmas* (2000), *Men In Black* (1997).

GUESS WHAT? Verne stands at just 2ft 8in tall and has body-doubled as Pinocchio and a baby gorilla.

QUOTABLE QUOTE: 'It's pretty difficult for me to go out in public anymore without friends around. I can cause a bit of a stampede. People are so generous in their attention, but crowds can be dangerous for me.'

JULIE WALTERS (MOLLY WEASLEY)

OTHER CREDITS: *Calendar Girls* (2003), *Billy Elliot* (2000), *Educating Rita* (1983)

GUESS WHAT? Julie originally trained as a nurse as her mother was dead set against her having an acting career.

QUOTABLE QUOTES: '[My mother] used to say to me, "No good will come of it, believe me. You'll end up in the gutter" – which turned out to be true, now and again.'

MARK WILLIAMS (ARTHUR WEASLEY)

OTHER CREDITS: *Agent Cody Banks 2: Destination London* (2004), *101 Dalmatians* (1996), *The Fast Show* (UK TV series).

GUESS WHAT? Canal-boat fan Mark also hosts a radio show called *The Tape-Recorded Highlights Of A Humble Bee.*

JULIAN GLOVER (VOICE OF ARAGOG)

OTHER CREDITS: *Star Wars: Episode V – The Empire Strikes Back* (1980), *For Your Eyes Only* (1981), *Indiana Jones And The Last Crusade* (1989)

GUESS WHAT? Julian had the horrible experience of seeing himself crumble into dust in *Indiana Jones And The Last Crusade* after his character drank from a false Holy Grail in pursuit of eternal life.

RIK MAYALL (PEEVES)

OTHER CREDITS: Numerous comic roles including Alan B'stard, Rik in *The Young Ones* and Lord Flashheart in *Blackadder II* and *IV*. He also played Adolf Hitler in *Churchill: The Hollywood Years* (2004)

GUESS WHAT? After a serious quad-bike accident in 1998, Rik says that a homemade card and a lucky charm sent by a young fan called Lara helped his recovery. His part in the first Harry Potter film ended up on the cutting-room floor during strenuous efforts to chop the length of the film.

QUOTABLE QUOTES: As Rik in *The Young Ones*: 'We *never* clean the toilet, Neil! That's what being a student is all about.'

ZOË WANAMAKER (MADAM HOOCH)

OTHER CREDITS: *Adrian Mole: The Cappuccino Years* (2001), *David Copperfield* (1999), *My Family* (UK TV comedy series).

GUESS WHAT? Despite having a perfect English accent, Zoë, the daughter of actor and director Sam Wanamaker, is actually a US citizen.

QUOTABLE QUOTES: 'I don't have the confidence to be a personality.'

JULIE CHRISTIE (MADAM ROSMERTA)

OTHER CREDITS: *Dragonheart* (1996), *Don't Look Now* (1973), *Doctor Zhivago* (1965)

GUESS WHAT? In 1995 Julie was voted one of the 100 sexiest stars of film history. She supports many good causes, including the Fairtrade Foundation and the Kurdish Human Rights Project.

QUOTABLE QUOTES: There aren't any because she hardly ever speaks to the press or public.

DAWN FRENCH (FAT LADY IN PAINTING)

OTHER CREDITS: UK TV series including *French And Saunders* and *The Vicar Of Dibley*. She was also the voice of Buttercup in *Watership Down* (1999) and starred in *David Copperfield* in the same year.

GUESS WHAT? She's one of the founders of Comic Relief, along with her husband, Lenny Henry, and supports its fundraising efforts. She also co-wrote two knitting books: *Big Knits* and *Great Big Knits*.

QUOTABLE QUOTES: 'Motherhood has tested me beyond belief.'

TIMOTHY SPALL (PETER PETTIGREW)

OTHER CREDITS: *The Last Samurai* (2003), *Chicken Run* (2000), *Secrets And Lies* (1996) and bricklayer Barry in the UK TV series *Auf Wiedersehen, Pet!*

GUESS WHAT? Timothy recovered from leukaemia after being diagnosed with the condition in 1996, although he has never spoken publicly about it. He is the father of Rafe Spall, who appeared in *The Calcium Kid* and *Shaun Of The Dead*.

Quotable quote: 'I'm not always fat, but when I'm thin people don't seem to notice. I'm seen as a fat person, no matter what shape I'm in.'

DAVID THEWLIS (PROFESSOR REMUS LUPIN)

Other credits: *Endgame* (2000), *The Big Lebowski* (1998), *Dragonheart* (1996).

GUESS WHAT? He's banned from China because of his role in the critical film *Seven Years In Tibet*, made in 1997. He and his girlfriend, Anna Friel, are mates with Sting and Trudie Styler.

QUOTABLE QUOTES: 'I've got loads of kiddie friends. If you say, "You'll never guess what I'm doing," and then tell them, they start screaming. And then you tell them, "You can come to the set and meet Harry Potter," and they get short of breath. It's worth it just for that.'

PAUL WHITEHOUSE (SIR CADOGAN)

OTHER CREDITS: *Kevin And Perry Go Large* (2000), *Finding Neverland* (2004), *The Fast Show* (UK TV series).

GUESS WHAT? Paul became famous after writing comedy for his chum Harry Enfield. He is also a keen angler.

QUOTABLE QUOTES: 'I'm not the kind of person who hankers after the celebrity world.'

RALPH FIENNES (LORD VOLDEMORT)

OTHER CREDITS: *Maid In Manhattan* (2002), *The Prince Of Egypt* (1998), *The English Patient* (1996)

GUESS WHAT? Ralph is older brother of actor Joseph Fiennes and the cousin of explorer Sir Ranulph Fiennes. His name is pronounced 'Rafe'.

QUOTABLE QUOTES: 'I am naturally drawn to dark roles.'

MIRANDA RICHARDSON (RITA SKEETER)

OTHER CREDITS: *The Phantom Of The Opera* (2004), *Churchill: The Hollywood Years* (2004), *Blackadder Back And Forth* (1999)

GUESS WHAT? Harry Potter is familiar territory for Richardson, who played Hermione in a spoof filmed in 2003 as part of the Comic Relief fundraising efforts, titled *Harry Potter And The Secret Chamberpot Of Azerbaijan*. Before she began acting, she wanted to be a vet.

QUOTABLE QUOTES: 'I'd be hopeless as a vet. I'm far too squeamish, far too emotional.'

FRANCES DE LA TOUR (MADAME MAXIME, HEADMISTRESS OF BEAUXBATONS)

OTHER CREDITS: *Strike It Rich* (1990), *Duet For One* (1981), *Rising Damp* (UK TV comedy series).

GUESS WHAT? She once played a female Hamlet and her brother, Andy, is also an actor.

QUOTABLE QUOTES: 'What the actor feels is important but what the actor feels about the part is not.'

DAVID TENNANT (BARTY CROUCH, JR)

Other credits: *He Knew He Was Right* (2004), *Blackpool* (2004), *Doctor Who* (TV series).

GUESS WHAT? David confesses that he'd like to impersonate Jarvis Cocker on an edition of *Celebrity Stars In Their Eyes*, a karaoke-style TV show.

QUOTABLE QUOTES: 'My earliest memory is of seeing Jon Pertwee regenerate into Tom Baker on *Doctor Who* and being entirely entranced. My desire to act came from watching the telly and wanting to be the people on there, wanting to tell stories.'

BRENDAN GLEESON (DEFENCE AGAINST THE DARK ARTS TEACHER MAD-EYE MOODY)

OTHER CREDITS: *Cold Mountain* (2003), *Gangs Of New York* (2002).

GUESS WHAT? An accomplished fiddle player, Brendan was a teacher at secondary school until he decided to throw in the day job and become an actor at the age of 34.

QUOTABLE QUOTES: 'The first time I went to see an agent in America, he told me, "You're too fat, too old, not good-looking enough" – that I'd never make it, basically.'

ROBERT HARDY (CORNELIUS FUDGE, MINISTER FOR MAGIC)

OTHER CREDITS: *Frankenstein* (1994), *An Ideal Husband* (1998), *Thunderpants* (2002)

GUESS WHAT? Although Hardy is most famous for being Siegfried Farnon in the televised and film versions of the James Herriot vet books, he has also played Winston Churchill four times. Away from the screen he's an expert on medieval weaponry, especially the longbow.

QUOTABLE QUOTES: 'Take each day as it comes, do everything you do to the best of your ability and try not to hurt others. I don't know if there is a secret to success. I think everyone has to find their own feet and achieve success on their own terms. If there was a magic formula, it would long ago have been bottled and sold.'

EMMA THOMPSON (PROFESSOR SYBILL TRELAWNEY)

OTHER CREDITS: *Love, Actually* (2003), *Angels In America* (2003), *Primary Colors* (1998)

GUESS WHAT? Emma, who is left-handed, is fluent in French and Spanish.

QUOTABLE QUOTES: 'I have a nervous breakdown in [*Harry Potter And The Prisoner Of Azkaban*], and in one scene I get to stand at the top of the stairs, waving an empty sherry bottle – which is, of course, a typical scene from my daily life, so it isn't much of a stretch.'

— CATALOGUE OF BEASTS AND CREATURES —

BASILISK
In mythology, the basilisk is the king of serpents, able to slaughter other snakes with a single hiss. According to descriptions of the beast provided by the Ancient Egyptians, it bore a white, crown-like mark on its head. The Roman archivist Pliny held that the destructive power of the basilisk was immense: 'It is believed that once one was killed with a spear by a man on horseback and the infection rising through the spear killed not only the rider but also the horse.' However, it was later theories suggesting that the ashes of a basilisk could turn silver into gold that focused the thoughts of future generations on it. During the Middle Ages, when optimists were known as alchemists and tried to turn base metals into gold, a dead basilisk was worth its weight in…well…gold.

BOGGART
According to the folklore of Yorkshire and Lancashire, a boggart is a mischievous spirit at the heart of all domestic disasters. It seems that they can be quite an asset around the house until they take offence at a mild rebuke or imagined insult, when their boundless energies are devoted to creating mishaps and mayhem. Troublesome boggarts might be wooed back by gifts of food or treats. Some boggarts are shape-shifters, occasionally appearing in the form of an animal. Sometimes the term 'boggart' is applied in the north of England to ghosts or poltergeists, while in America boggarts are better known as bogeymen.

COCKATRICE
An unhealthy blend of dragon and rooster with killer looks and fatally bad breath. The word 'cockatrice' is also used as another name for a basilisk.

DEMENTORS
The guards of the creepy wizard prison Azkaban. Close contact with the Dementors is as bad a punishment as a spell behind bars. Beneath their flowing robes they are slimy in appearance, and their presences makes happiness and hope evaporate. Although they appear to have heightened senses, the Dementors are actually blind. Author JK Rowling created them as a personification of depression. According to Lord Voldemort, the Dementors are his 'natural allies' and will join him. This is precisely what Dumbledore and others have predicted.

DOXIES
A household pet in a similar vein to cockroaches, the Doxies at Grimmauld Place are considered both a physical menace and a health hazard. By dictionary definition, a doxy is a courtesan – that is, a woman living with a rich man –

and the term was once used to indicate a woman with loose morals. The word is taken from the Dutch word *docke*, meaning 'doll'.

FAIRIES

Many children grow up with the firm belief that fairies are the good guys. Take the three fairies in the Disney version of *Sleeping Beauty*, who just couldn't do enough for the heroine and went all a-shiver in the face of the evil witch.

Alas, this is another example of a corporation hijacking that has marked our subconscious, because there's plenty of material out there that says fairies aren't the likeable, lively, good-hearted types that cartoon makers would have us believe. Nor do they like nothing better than squatting on a flowerhead for any passing artist, as greetings card manufacturers imply. What about the long-held belief that they were responsible for stealing human babies and that anyone who spied on them doing so would be blinded? Not so cute now, eh?

Sightings of fairies declined dramatically in the latter half of the 20th century, which could be put down to the effect of pollution and the urban sprawl destroying the typical fairy habitat, or an epidemic of scepticism. However, the belief in fairies remains strong among all gap-toothed youngsters with an eye for quick money, who are prepared to welcome a fairy – no matter how gruesome – into their bedrooms to exchange a lost tooth for hard cash.

GIANT

British people have been quick to believe in the existence of giants. After all, images of them have been etched into the grasslands for centuries, the most famous being the Cerne Abbas giant in Dorset. Also known as the Rude Man for the depiction of his outsized anatomy, the Cerne Abbas giant is 180ft (55m) tall and wields a club that measures 120ft (36.5m) in length.

No mention is made of this outline giant in literature until the mid-18th century, but the date of its creation is unknown. There's speculation that he is a representation of the god Hercules cut at the end of the second century, when the Roman emperor Commodus, who ruled Britain, believed he was a reincarnation of the big man and set the religious agenda accordingly. Another story says that mischievous monks cut the figure as a joke against their abbot. Locally, word has it that a real giant sent by the Danish was killed there and the event was celebrated by drawing the dead guy in chalk, not least to warn other outsized visitors of their sure fate. The giant has since been adopted as a fertility symbol.

Hagrid might be your favourite (half) giant but he's only one of many over-sized characters to grace the pages of children's literature. The most famous and best-loved giant, pre-Harry Potter, was the BFG, created by Roald Dahl. This big, friendly giant stood out among other giants for his kindness to little orphan Sophie. However, the usual depiction of giants was of tall, ugly and intellectually challenged creatures of an unusually violent disposition.

Take the giant in *Jack And The Beanstalk*, best remembered for his chant of 'Fee, fi, fo, fum' and his odd yearning for bread made from human bones (yuk!). He was sufficiently slow-witted to be fooled by a boy, as were numerous other giants according to folklore. Their public image is in the balance, as it remains to be seen whether JK Rowling has them as goodies or bad guys.

HINKYPUNK

Also known as a will o' the wisp, a hinkypunk is either a luminous fairy or one carrying a torch or lantern. They are famous for appearing at a distance over marshes or other bleak countryside. If you're lost on the road, never ask one for directions as they will entice you into the local marshlands, where you will come to a sticky end.

CENTAUR

A centaur has the head and torso of a man and the lower body of a horse, which gives it six limbs and an ability to gallop. They look just like the illustration for the star-sign Sagittarius. Centaurs are straight out of Greek mythology, in which they are largely represented as overly boisterous and not awfully clever. They knocked about with satyrs, rather less appealing creatures who were half men and half goat. The odds are that centaur stories began when the Greeks – who were not horsey people – first encountered tribes of rampaging nomads on horseback and found it difficult to distinguish between the rider's legs and the animal's back. Anyway, one of the centaurs did gain a reputation for wisdom. His name was Chiron and he became a tutor to some of the great Greek heroes, including Achilles.

This mythological strand re-emerges in *Harry Potter And The Order Of The Phoenix* when the centaur Firenze begins work as a teacher at Hogwarts and gives lessons to our own modern heroes.

TROLL

According to author Newt Scamander, the average troll stands in the region of 12ft (3.6m) tall and weighs in excess of a tonne. They are reported as being strong and stupid, unpredictable, incoherent and possibly incontinent. Trolls come in three varieties: mountain, forest and river.

Trolls have a fearfully poor reputation. Indeed, they are one of the few creatures that have made even goats look sophisticated. Remember how the three billy goats gruff crossed the bridge controlled by a river troll and evaded capture by promising him a larger helping of goat coming along behind? The troll was so greedy that he permitted the first two goats to head for the lush mountain grass and held back for the third and biggest one. Without ado, the third goat tossed him into the river, where he drowned. Unfortunately, it appears that trolls do not possess the intellectual capacity to learn from their mistakes.

In her book *A History Of Magic*, Bathilda Bagshot recalls a 14th-century wizards' summit called to confirm the definition of 'beasts', which was also attended by trolls. She revealed that the riled trolls broke up the meeting – literally: 'A dozen or so trolls began to smash apart the chamber with their clubs…'

Although the source of their information remains unverified, the makers of the hit movie *Elf* believe that trolls experience difficulty with toilet training.

BANSHEE
A fairy, typically of Irish descent, that attends to a particular family, rather like a house elf. A banshee can appear in the form of a young lady, a matronly woman, an old hag or even an animal. They have the gift of foresight and are best known for wailing at high pitch as a warning of imminent death. (The fact that the shrill sound was alone sufficient to induce death seems to have bypassed the myth-makers of ancient Ireland.) The word 'banshee' is derived from the Celtic words *bean* ('woman') and *sidhe* ('fairy').

CORNISH PIXIE
In Harry Potter land, Cornish pixies are electric blue and a rather diminutive 8in (20cm) in height. This isn't a description of the customary West Country pixies, or 'piscies', who wear green garb, a pointy hat and have a passion for dancing in the moonlight.

OGRE
Large, smelly and thoroughly unprepossessing beasts, ogres have struck fear into the hearts of villagers and maidens down the centuries.

In the 21st century, however, ogres have been subject to a major makeover, thanks to the arrival of Shrek. He is enormous and growly, like every other ogre you've ever known, but in the first two films of a series bearing his name he is revealed to have a heart of gold. His reputation is also enhanced for an heroic tolerance of his sidekick, Donkey, architect of such irritating sayings as 'Are we there yet?'

GNOMES

Harry first encounters gnomes at the Weasleys' Burrow, where they are considered a garden pest. Most of us are more familiar with the inanimate kind of gnome that tends to inhabit our own gardens, sometimes fishing, sometimes pushing a barrow. Even these curious creatures have the capacity for adventure. There are numerous documented cases of garden gnomes heading off overseas for extended holidays, sending postcards and even photographs back to their perplexed owners.

The first such occurrence is believed to have been in Sydney, Australia, in the mid-1980s. There the gnomes' owners swiftly received a postcard purporting to be from the absent ornament on vacation in Queensland. He returned two weeks later bearing a tan, which was later revealed to be brown shoe polish.

When her three gnomes vanished, Barbara Austin of Greensboro, North Carolina, was left a note that read simply, 'Gone travelin'. Back later.' And indeed, they did travel widely in the 50 days they were away, covering some 11,000 miles (17,700km) through 28 states, into both Canada and Mexico. When they returned, they brought with them a map and a photo album that pictured them at major landmarks.

Much of the charm of gnome-napping was dispelled by the radical French group Le Front de Libération des Nains de Jardin (the Garden Gnome Liberation Front), a group that claimed to have freed some 6,000 in the months after it was formed in 1997. Many were returned to the forest, where they were found in clusters, trying to return to their 'roots'.

GRINDYLOW

An ugly water demon commonly blamed for pulling children into water holes and rivers.

KAPPA

An inscrutable oriental water demon with a taste for blood.

SALAMANDER

In mythology, a lizard-like creature that lives in fires and feeds on flames and whose blood is highly valued as a cure-all. In reality, the salamander is an amphibian rather than a lizard and there are numerous different types of varying size. Bizarrely, the animal is capable of regrowing lost limbs.

WEREWOLF

The name comes from the Olde English words *wer* ('man') and *wulf* ('wolf') and has struck terror into the hearts of men for centuries. A werewolf was allegedly a man transformed into a wolf (customarily under the light of a full moon) and who then preyed on human victims until dawn's first rays.

Could one of your neighbours be the local werewolf? The man most likely to transform into a werewolf could, it was said, be distinguished by fierce red eyes, bushy eyebrows that meet in the middle and claw-like fingers. Also, anyone unfortunate enough to drink from a haunted stream or a wolf's footprint or to wear something belonging to an existing werewolf would themselves become enchanted.

In the Middle Ages, people believed wholeheartedly in the existence of werewolves. Richard Rowland's 1605 book *Restitution Of Decayed Intelligence*, explains: 'Werewolves are certaine sorcerers, who having annointed their bodies with an ointment which they make by the instinct of the Devil and putting on a certain enchanted girdel do not only unto the view of others seem as wolves but to their own thinking have both the shape and the natures of wolves so long as they weare the said girdel.'

Curiously, the werewolf theory had been debunked centuries earlier. Roman writer Pliny the Elder declared, 'That men may be transformed into wolves and restored again to their former shape we must confidently believe to be a lewd lie or else give credit to all those tales which we have for so many ages found to be mere fabulous untruths.'

YETI – SEE PAGE 165

PHOENIX

Fawkes the phoenix is Professor Dumbledore's beloved pet bird. Perched in the headmaster's office, Fawkes surprises Harry by bursting into flames and burning until he turns into a pile of ashes. The phoenix is in fact a mythological bird that was particularly prominent in Ancient Egypt, where it represented resurrection from death and immortality. The Greek writer Herodotus described phoenixes as being something like an eagle in size, with red and golden plumage. The phoenix's lifespan was said to be around 500 years, and when one bird was consumed by fire, a new one would arise from the ashes it left behind. The name Fawkes is of course inspired by Guy Fawkes, the 17th-century gunpowder plotter who schemed to blow up the British Houses of Parliament as a protest against Protestantism. The ardent Catholic was captured and horribly tortured before being put to death. Each year his passing is marked on 5 November, Bonfire Night.

DWARVES

Although famous mainly for their appearance in a Walt Disney cartoon with the house-cleaning fiend Snow White – the first feature-length animation of its kind ever made, back in 1937 – mythical dwarves actually have a far richer history.

In reality, sometimes humans grow up to be abnormally small. There may be a variety of causes of this, including hormone deficiency, lack of decent nutrition, heart disease, emotional deprivation or a condition known as *achonodroplasia*, which results in short limbs. Although small people are often referred to as dwarves, the term is inaccurate and insulting.

Just for the record (and because no one can ever remember them all), the names of the Walt Disney seven are Grumpy, Sneezy, Bashful, Dopey, Doc, Sleepy and Happy.

UNICORN

A favourite feature of myths and legends, the unicorn is in essence a single-horned horse that was originally believed to inhabit India. In Western stories, it is generally represented as being wild and fleet while Eastern tales hold it to be a calmer creature that brings with it good fortune.

Of course, there's no evidence that unicorns ever existed. It is assumed that unicorn tales were inspired by horned antelope, the rhinoceros or even the sea-going narwhal. However, vivid descriptions of them have been recorded down the centuries, one of the earliest being written in 398 BC by the Greek Ctesias, who declared that unicorns lived in India, were the size of a horse and had a white body, red head, blue eyes and a horn protruding from their forehead measuring about 20in (50cm).

In the Middle Ages, the mystical properties of the unicorn were well known. After the story of a poisoned waterhole being purified by the horn of a unicorn became popular, it was the heartfelt desire of every king and baron to drink from a severed unicorn horn, paranoid as they were about the effects of drugs put into their food or wine by ambitious courtiers.

The unicorn is also associated with chastity or virginity. Also, from medieval times comes a story that a unicorn, too fast and wild to be captured by a hunter, willingly laid its head in the lap of a lonely maiden under a tree. Alas for him, she whipped out a knife as soon as it slept and cut off its horn, presumably to sell to the highest bidder. The beast's link with Britain's moneyed classes continues, as it appears on the crest of the royal family.

DRAGON

As with their views on unicorns, the East and West have different perceptions of dragons. In China, dragons are all full of goodness, greatness and godliness. The fantastical creatures are fêted for their wisdom, worshipped for the protection they offer against evil spirits and honoured for their unearthly potency.

Such is the faith of oriental people in dragons that a 13th-century Cambodian king spent his nights in a golden tower, where he communed with a nine-headed dragon, a beast that he believed really ruled his land.

There are nine different types of Chinese dragon, each with specific characteristics; one is deaf, for example, while another is fond of music. Sometimes one is a bit fierce, but they are mostly a benign bunch who help to make life tick along like clockwork.

In the West, an altogether more bloodthirsty variety of dragon has made its home in children's stories. Looking something like an outsized lizard, such a beast is best known for its fire-breathing abilities and its tastes for valuable treasure and human flesh. A habit of running off with beautiful maidens has led many dragons to meet their deaths at the swords of handsome princes.

There's nothing to say that such a creature as a dragon ever existed, and yet there's anecdotal evidence around even today to suggest that some manner of dragon once lived, or perhaps still does. The most famous example of an oft-spotted dragon is the so-called Loch Ness Monster, although highly scientific searches for evidence of the water-going Nessie have come up with zip. (In the Harry Potter books, author Newt Scamander believes that this is a rogue kelpie that openly flouts Clause 73 of the International Statute of Wizarding Secrecy, which governs the concealment of magical beings from Muggles.)

The Old English term for a dragon was *wyrm*, and the looping headland extending from the Welsh county of west Glamorgan is thus called Wormshead for its likeness to a dragon's body. Reflecting a commonly held folk tradition, dragon artefacts, including their skin, are greatly prized in the wizarding world. Even the overtly optimistic Hagrid realises he's made a mistake when he takes on Norbert the dragon as a pet. As Hermione once put it, 'Dragon's blood's amazingly magical but you wouldn't want a dragon for a pet, would you?'

GOBLIN

Looking like stunted, discoloured humans, goblins are saddled with an image of wasters and troublemakers. In fact, they can be relatively industrious – just look at the way they keep Gringotts Bank in order – while their reputation for heavy drinking appears to have been exaggerated. Griphook the Goblin at Gringotts Bank has the happy knack of being able to open vaults with a gentle brush of his hand. In Celtic tradition, goblins are better known as brownies, while other cultures brand them as sprites.

SPHINX

Harry encounters a sphinx during his final challenge in the Triwizard Tournament. With the body of a large lion and the head of a woman with a mysterious smile, she delivers a riddle that he must solve before he can progress, warning him sternly that, if he answers the riddle wrongly, she will attack him.

Sphinxes are usually associated with Ancient Egypt, primarily because of the outsized sculpture of one that stands alongside the pyramids at Giza. This one actually has a man's head (although the beard has long since been lost) and a lion's body. Indeed, sphinxes in mythology have been depicted as somewhat surprising head-and-body combos, often with wings. Yet, however bizarre their appearance, they are inevitably associated with wisdom and strength.

LEPRECHAUN

Leprechauns are a mischievous bunch of little people from Ireland for whom the word *craic* (Irish for 'having a laugh') was created. We know from the Harry Potter series that they tricked various wizards and would-be wizards into accepting their gold, which vanished a few hours later. It's a typical leprechaun gag that might cause embarrassment but doesn't actually harm anyone.

Leprechauns usually stand about 2ft tall and wear distinctive garb that's generally green and includes a cocked hat and leather apron (they are renowned shoe-makers). Their inclination to keep a pot of gold has made them the prey of treasure hunters over the years, but those predators will find that the little man disappears before their eyes if they fail to hold his gaze. The existence or otherwise of the leprechaun is generally celebrated on St Patrick's Day, March 17.

HIPPOGRIFF – SEE PAGE 172

GARGOYLE

These are carved stone waterspouts on grand houses and cathedrals, named for a French serpent named Gargouille. Indeed, the first carvings of such beasts were made in his horrible likeness. A gargoyle guards the entrance to Dumbledore's office.

— THE SCIENCE OF SPELLS A–Z —

'The universe is not only queerer than we suppose but queerer than we *can* suppose.'

– Professor JBS Haldane, pioneer of genetics

Prof Haldane had it about right. Science – especially the wackier bits concerning how the universe works – gets weirder by the minute. Fortunately, that won't be a problem once time travel is discovered because scientists can then rewind those minutes to get more thinking time, as per the time turner. All clear so far? Thought not.

It's fair to say that the worlds of Hogwarts and modern science are more closely related than you might think. In fact, to say you don't *believe* in magic is a bit like saying you don't *believe* in science. Neither can explain everything. In fact, very often they can't even explain themselves. If you doubt this, try reading the work of the mathematical genius Kurt Gödel (but take a deep breath first!).

On 17 November 1930 Gödel became the first person to demonstrate that certain mathematical statements can be neither proved nor disproved. This came as a shattering blow to all those brainbox boffins who, until then, had thought that they could answer every properly phrased question on a true-or-false basis. By 'properly phrased', they meant that you can't ask, 'My boiled egg was runny this morning – true or false?' but you *can* ask, 'My 155mm-circumference boiled egg had a penetration unit of 60 after it was fully immersed in boiling water for three minutes – true or false?' Mathematicians would be happy with the latter query, because they could use data from previous egg-boiling experiments to solve an equation.

Theoretical maths and quantum physics are a quite different pan of eggs, however, because experimental data isn't always available. Gödel showed that scientific theory is a system of thought containing unprovable statements, which therefore must, by definition, require a leap of faith. And if you can have faith in science, you can have faith in magic. As the mathematicians might say, QED – which, by the way, is short for 'Quod erat demonstrandum' in Latin, which in turn translates as 'That which was to be demonstrated' (or 'See? Told you so') in English.

This guide looks at some of the common spells, objects and experiences from Harry's world and considers how science produces, or might one day produce, similar effects. Remember, some of the following dabbles in the truly bizarre world of quantum physics and theories based on *current* knowledge. On the subject of time travel, for instance, the question isn't so much whether we could make a time machine but whether the laws of physics would let it work! If there are bits you don't understand, that's probably because I don't understand them either. And that proves that Professor Haldane was right!

A IS FOR APPARATE
HOGWARTS VERSION
As every trainee wizard knows, apparating is a right carry-on. It involves the risk of *splinching* (materialising half of your body at one destination and the other half elsewhere) plus the bother of applying for a licence from the Department of Magical Transportation. However, most wizards – especially those with something to sell – use it as a method of choice, and Fred and George use it more than most.

MUGGLES VERSION
Apparating seems to be a form of teleportation – the thing they do in *Star Trek* when Captain Kirk says, 'Beam me up, Scotty,' and disappears in a blob of fuzzy lights. Surprisingly, teleportation is now accepted as a scientific possibility, thanks to experiments conducted by the University of Aarhus (among others) in which scientists have managed to teleport atoms by 'entangling' them using a beam of light. Teleporting humans would involve clones and atom division and, it seems to me, a whole pile of luck. The one thing that might cause a problem is something known as Heisenberg's Uncertainty Principle, which dictates that, while you can know an atom's location or the direction in which it's travelling, you can't know both at once, which would make reassembling the constituent parts of the apparator well-nigh impossible – at least, by today's reckoning.

See? I told you this stuff was tricky! Muggles are way behind wizards on this one.

B IS FOR BLAST-ENDED SKREWT
HOGWARTS VERSION
Hogwarts students in Harry's year suffered sore fingers as a result of handling – or rather mishandling – Blast-Ended Skrewts. However, although they are a fascinating element of Hagrid's Care of Magical Creatures class, the fiery rear-end action that propels the beasts forward isn't particularly magical. And we're not talking about *that* kind of rear-end action.

MUGGLES VERSION
Muggles have long had their own version of the Skrewt in the form of the bombardier beetle, or *Stenaptinus insignis*. This amazing little creature fends off predators by forcing hydroquinone and hydrogen peroxide from one chamber in its abdomen into a second chamber, where they mix with enzymes. The

ensuing chemical reaction heats this solution to boiling point, the hydroquinone is converted to toxic benzoquinone, a mini-explosion occurs and a hot, toxic liquid is sprayed at the enemy via two directional pipes at the rate of 500 pulses per second. It all happens very fast. Don't mess with this beetle.

C IS FOR CURSES
HOGWARTS VERSION
Cursing is considered bad form among respectable wizards, although Voldemort and his cronies don't let that worry them. In fact, many curses, such as the Cruciatus, Furnunculus, Impedimenta and Locomotor Mortis, bear some likenesses to Muggle equivalents. Perhaps the best example for comparison is the Imperius curse, a so-called 'unforgivable' curse because the caster can use it to control a victim's mind and body.

MUGGLES VERSION
The closest thing to the Imperius in Muggles-land is hypnotism, a form of mind control. No one really knows how this works, but scientists reckon that there must be an explanation or it would count as magic, and that would be terrible! Mother Nature has also produced some fantastic feats of brain control lower down the food chain, particularly the lancet liver fluke *Dicrocoelium dendriticum*, a cattle parasite that starts its life cycle inside ants. The ants get infected through eating cowpats (nice), but the problem for *D. dendriticum* lies in persuading cows to eat ants so that its life cycle can continue. It sneakily manages this by manipulating ant brains. When temperatures drop during the evening, the insects feel compelled to climb blades of grass and hang on with their mandibles. There they patiently wait to be eaten by grazing cattle, thus ensuring a new batch of parasites. No fluke with this life cycle, then!

D IS FOR DIAGON ALLEY
HOGWARTS VERSION
When Harry first visits Diagon Alley with Hagrid, he enters via a walled courtyard at the back of the Leaky Cauldron pub. Hagrid counts the bricks above a dustbin – 'three up…two across…' – then taps the wall with his umbrella and an archway magically appears. Harry and Hagrid walk through and the bricks re-form behind them.

MUGGLES VERSION
Could the wall be a wormhole? According to renowned cleverdick Albert Einstein's General Theory of Relativity, time and space are treated on an equal footing and it's theoretically possible to create gateways between different parts of the universe, or even different universes. One idea is that, if you could enter a black hole (that's a chunk of space with such powerful gravity that not

even light escapes), you could travel along a wormhole and be spewed out of a 'white hole' at another time or place. The big problem lies in stopping yourself from being crushed into oblivion long before you could swallow the travel-sickness tablets. But remember, they said aeroplanes would never fly!

E IS FOR ERISED, MIRROR OF
HOGWARTS VERSION

This should really be listed under M, but I've already got an M so I've cheated a bit. The Mirror of Erised projects a viewer's deepest desire, which in Harry's case was a longing to be reunited with his parents. It deceived his brain into believing that the images it showed him were real so that, when Harry saw his dead mother standing beside him, he reached out to touch her.

MUGGLES VERSION

The bewilderment Harry feels is similar to that experienced by stroke victims suffering from something known as *mirror agnosia*, or *Looking Glass syndrome*. Case studies at the University of California showed how patients suffering from this condition bumped their hands against a mirror as they tried to reach an object behind the glass. A somewhat different – and emotionally painful – brain disorder is the bereavement hallucination, whereby grieving people believe that they've seen a deceased partner or loved one. As for detecting desire, it might one day be possible for a scanner to record and interpret brainwaves indicating desire. The result could be projected as a virtual-reality image. Perhaps it will be called the Erised effect.

F IS FOR FLUFFY
HOGWARTS VERSION

Fluffy is the monstrous three-headed dog with rolling eyes that Hagrid claims to have bought as a pet from a 'Greek chappie' down the pub and helps to guard the Philosopher's Stone. JK Rowling seems to be likening Fluffy to Cerberus, the three-headed hound from Greek mythology that guards the entrance to the Kingdom of the Dead and can be also be lulled to sleep with music.

MUGGLES VERSION

It has been possible to create multi-headed animals artificially in laboratories for at least 80 years. Early experiments involved grafting 'organiser tissue' from one frog embryo to another, thus creating a creature with two heads. More recently, scientists have found the fittingly named Cerberus gene, which, when injected into a frog embryo, produces the same result. The process would be trickier in larger mammals such as like dogs, but still feasible. It all throws up some hard questions for scientists, hardest of which is, should an experiment be done just because it *can* be done?

G IS FOR GIANT SQUID
HOGWARTS VERSION
Hogwarts' resident giant squid lives in the school lake, where it enjoys occasional treats of left-over toast, saved from breakfast by pupils.

MUGGLES VERSION
In a rare case of reality outdoing fantasy, the *Architeuthis* squid ('architeuthis' is Greek for 'chief squid') is the world's largest and most advanced invertebrate (ie a creature with no backbone). It is so shy that no live adult of the species has ever been seen. However, from studying dead ones dragged up in fishing nets, we know that they weigh at least a ton, are 60ft long and have eyes the size of dinner plates. Scarily, in 1753 the Bishop of Bergen in Germany described one as a sea monster 'full of arms' and big enough to crush a warship.

H IS FOR HAT (AS IN SORTING)
HOGWARTS VERSION
The Sorting Hat assesses the inner mind and characteristics of Hogwarts pupils to decide which house would suit them best. It has a momentary dilemma with Harry, briefly judging him a potential Slytherin, before assigning him to Gryffindor.

MUGGLES VERSION
Muggles have recently made giant strides in developing mind-reading machines. The most promising method is to use a process known as *magneto-encephalography* (or MEG for short), which records the minuscule magnetic fields created by electrical messages as they pass through brain cells. To do this, MEG relies on the use of a superconducting quantum interference device, or SQUID, which fits around your head – just like the Sorting Hat. This machine converts everything into voltage readings that can then be measured and deciphered. Magneto-encephalographists can't yet read your precise thoughts, but they *can* tell what kind of instructions your brain is dishing out – such as 'play the piano' or 'eat a Mars bar' – simply by looking at a printout of your brainwaves. There is also a technique known as *transcranial magnetic stimulation* that can make you move uncontrollably by zapping your brain with pulses of magnetic energy (shades of the Imperius curse here) while also making you temporarily cleverer! SQUIDs, by the way, are the most sensitive measuring devices in science…which is just as well, because the human brain is easily the most complex structure in the known universe.

I IS FOR INVISIBILITY
HOGWARTS VERSION
Invisibility is a spectacularly (or should that be unspectacularly?) useful wizarding skill, and there are several ways of conjuring it up. Harry's invisibility

cloak – woven from the hair of a demiguise beast and bequeathed to him by his father – works as long as he's properly tucked underneath it, while Arthur Weasley's flying Ford Anglia has an invisibility booster button on the dashboard that generates a magical field. Then there's Dumbledore, who reveals that he doesn't need a cloak to make himself disappear and can spot others who merely *think* they've disappeared. Finally, there's the hard-to-find *Invisible Book Of Invisibility*, which would probably explain everything if only readers could see what the author was getting at. As it happens, though, the art of invisibility is somewhat elusive, it appears. Or rather doesn't appear. Or something.

MUGGLES VERSION

Muggles scientists, especially those who enjoy practical jokes, have for centuries dreamed of inventing an invisibility machine. The best effort so far has come from British, Canadian and German boffins who have fixed flexible videos screens – or 'smart skins' – to the front of military trucks. Mini cameras then project the background scene onto these screens with the aim of blending the truck into its surroundings. Strictly speaking, this is really a sneaky form of camouflage. Some people, however, believe that in 1943 American scientists managed to make an entire warship, the USS *Eldridge*, disappear in what was supposedly known as the Philadelphia Experiment. Supporters of this idea reckon that the ship was immersed in an immensely strong magnetic field that caused it to disappear, teleport through a space-time warp (see 'A' and 'D' above) and later reappear in the same spot. Probably a lot of fuss about nothing!

J IS FOR JELLIFICATION

HOGWARTS VERSION

When Professor Lockhart tries to mend Harry's arm in *Harry Potter And The Chamber Of Secrets*, he blunders and uses a jellification spell rather than the mending charm he had intended. Fortunately, Madam Pomfrey comes to the rescue, administering a cup of Skele-Gro potion with the ominous observation that 'regrowing bones is a nasty business'. Indeed, the regrowth of Harry's bones causes him agony.

MUGGLES VERSION

Bone loss is a very real problem for sufferers of diseases like osteoporosis and can occur quickly (though not as quickly as Lockhart managed it) in low-gravity conditions. This could be a big problem for astronauts on long missions – for instance, in orbiting space-stations. Fortunately, researchers have discovered that 'bone-growing' cells called *osteoblasts* can be stimulated through the use of low-level electrical fields or through an injection of special proteins to induce rapid bone growth. There is also good evidence to show that artificially vibrating the legs can increase bone density by up to 30 per cent.

K IS FOR KNIGHT BUS
HOGWARTS VERSION

The triple-decker Knight Bus has an uncanny knack of appearing out of thin air and negotiating impossibly narrow routes in order to fulfil its role as 'emergency transport for the stranded witch or wizard'. It can supposedly go anywhere on land, and buildings and benches simply squeeze themselves out of its way.

MUGGLES VERSION

You won't be surprised to learn that Muggles can offer nothing remotely close to the Knight Bus. It travels at close to the speed of light (you'll recall that Stan Shunpike spills Harry's hot chocolate as the bus moves abruptly from Anglesea [*sic*] to Aberdeen), and that means some weird stuff is bound to happen.

Einstein's Special Theory of Relativity shows that time and distance alter as you approach the speed at which light travels in a vacuum (186,000 miles per hour), and so someone at a fixed point watching a spaceship travel 25,000 light years* would have to *live* for 25,000 years. However, to a traveller actually *on* the spaceship the journey would seem like no time at all. Many Muggle boffins are convinced that we'll never travel close to light speed, although science doesn't have a great track record of successfully predicting cans and can'ts. Until quite recently, for instance, it was thought that nothing could travel faster than 186,000mph, but now experts at the NEC Research Institute in Princeton, New Jersey, have sent a pulse of light through a chamber prepared with caesium gas at *300 times* normal light speed. The main part of the pulse left the chamber before it even entered, which theoretically means that it's possible to see something happen before it actually happens. If you think that's mind-boggling, remember that the laws of quantum physics allow things to appear from nowhere and to happen for no reason. So if a bench can squeeze itself out of the Knight Bus's way, there's a simple explanation for this. It just can.

L IS FOR LUPIN, PROFESSOR
HOGWARTS VERSION

It can be beastly being a werewolf. At least one Hogwarts character goes through this agonising transformation once a month under the full moon. Only his wolfsbane potion ensures that his condition is kept under control.

MUGGLES VERSION

Lycanthropy is a well-known mental disorder in which a Muggle becomes

---

*A light year is a measure of the distance travelled by a beam of light in a year. Think lots of noughts.

convinced he's a werewolf. This is naturally very different to actually *being* a werewolf but still deeply unpleasant for the Muggle concerned. It's also possible to look like a werewolf if you suffer from a very rare genetic disorder called *congenital generalised hypertrichosis*, which was identified by the University of Guadalajara in 1984 and which causes excessive hair growth on the face and upper body. The condition is thought to be caused by the re-awakening of a long-dormant gene possessed by our early ancestors.

M IS FOR MAGICAL MESS REMOVER
HOGWARTS VERSION
Fans of the Quidditch World Cup are treated to advertisements that magically appear on the pitch as though written by an invisible giant. One of these reads, 'Mrs Skower's All-Purpose Magical Mess-Remover: No Pain, No Stain.'

MUGGLES VERSION
Modern household biological detergents rely heavily on enzymes, such as subtilisin, which work by dissolving the proteins in a stain into smaller pieces, making them easier to wash off. The advert on the Quidditch pitch suggests that Mrs Skower's potion works without the need for any additional input, which is probably just as well. Wizards getting involved with washing machines sounds like a recipe for disaster!

N IS FOR NIFFLERS
HOGWARTS VERSION
Nifflers are fluffy, black, mole-like creatures with a love of bright, shiny or sparkling things. They seem to have fantastic eyesight, which makes them useful for hunting down lost objects such as jewellery or Dumbledore's spectacles.

MUGGLES VERSION
Experiments at the University of Basel in Switzerland have shown that tweaking a particular gene in flies can produce eye-like structures on legs, antennae and even wings. By introducing a gene called Pax 6 (which causes eye defects in mice) into fruit flies and squid, the scientists made them grow eyes similar to those found on ordinary houseflies. This area of research makes people uncomfortable because (a) it smacks of playing God and (b) it seems creepily similar to classic sci-fi/horror film *The Fly*, in which mad scientists turns himself partially into an insect. But maybe this is good news for Muggle skinflints, who one day might be able to send specially trained, multi-eyed mice under the floorboards to hunt for coins.

O IS FOR OCCLUMENCY
HOGWARTS VERSION

Occlumency is the art of magically defending the mind against invasion or inquisition. It works by suppressing thought and emotion, denying the mind-reader a chance to uncover tell-tale titbits. Harry has some basic occlumency, and Dumbledore knows enough of the subject to teach it, but Severus Snape – who survived as a spy in the Death Eaters' camp under the nose of Voldemort himself – is the daddy.

MUGGLES VERSION

There are plenty of psychological tests and techniques that are supposed to expose a fibber. Sweating, avoidance of eye contact, repeated contradictions, hand-to-face movements – all of these have been cited by psychologists as indicators that you've told a whopper. However, they could also have innocent explanations. You might be hot, for instance, or you might not *like* making eye contact with strangers. You might be nervous or unsure. You might have an itchy spot on your chin!

In an attempt to make everything more…well…*scientific*, an American named William Moulton Marston invented the polygraph, a lie-detector machine that hooks up to a blood-pressure sensor on your arm, a wire on your fingers (to measure sweating) and rubber straps around your tummy (to monitor breathing). Interrogation starts with a series of control questions that calibrate your normal responses. Then the probing begins and your physical reactions appear as squiggles on a piece of graph paper. Polygraph opponents reckon that the machine has, at best, a 70 per cent success rate and simply indicates an emotional reaction. You can apparently beat it by holding your breath, clenching your arm muscles or pricking your foot on a tack hidden in your shoe. So *that's* Snape's secret?

P IS FOR PATRONUS

HOGWARTS VERSION

This charm protects a wizard against Dementors. The caster conjures it from the tip of his or her wand by concentrating on happy thoughts and crying, 'Expecto patronum!' at just the right moment. Each Patronus is unique to its wizard (Harry's is a stag), and because it has no concept of despair, the Dementors' destructive mind games are rendered ineffective.

MUGGLES VERSION

Every Muggle occasionally suffers a Dementor-friendly bad hair day, and one psychological antidote to the blues is to think yourself happy. This isn't a new idea; a book titled *The Power Of Positive Thinking* by Norman Peale has sold more than 20 million copies in 41 languages since it was first published half a century ago. According to a study at Harvard University in America, positive thinking seems particularly important for older Muggles. Researchers at the university flashed positive words (such as 'wise' and 'alert') at one group of elderly participants and negative words ('senile' and 'incompetent') at another. The positive group were later shown to be significantly better at memory tests, providing proof that positive thinking is the Muggle version of the Patronus charm.

Q IS FOR QUIDDITCH

HOGWARTS VERSION

Quidditch is the sport of choice for all broomstick lovers, but Hogwarts freshers must learn to fly before they try. Harry proves to be a natural stick-jockey, needing no instruction to outmanoeuvre Draco Malfoy in a breathtaking early duel, but the likes of Hermione Granger and Neville Longbottom initially struggle to get their brooms up. In their case, something like a 'broom-booster' would have been handy – and, funnily enough, Muggles are trying to invent that very thing.

MUGGLES VERSION

What Quidditch novices really need in those tricky first lessons is an anti-gravity machine. Muggle scientists have spent years trying to switch off gravity, and if they ever manage it then the implications are awesome. A spacecraft would barely need a nudge – say, the kick-off technique used by broomstick riders – to travel into space from a planet's surface. In 1992, a Russian researcher named Evgeny Podkletnov claimed to have reduced the weight of various objects, from ceramics to wood, by two per cent. He achieved this by placing them over a cooled, magnetically suspended, superconducting* 12in ceramic disc, which was spun using alternating electrical currents. The faster it turned, the greater the reduction in gravitational force. Two per cent might not sound like much, but Podkletnov's achievement encouraged NASA to test the idea further.

R IS FOR RIDDIKULUS

HOGWARTS VERSION

The Riddikulus charm is used to repel boggarts, those unnerving creatures that can sense a wizard's innermost fear and promptly turn into it. The charm forces a boggart to turn into something its victim finds funny, hence when Neville sees it as Professor Snape he manages to dress the 'Snape' in women's clothes. That incident, during Professor Lupin's first Defence Against the Dark Arts class, sounds something like a case of mass hallucination.

MUGGLES VERSION

As far as mass hallucinations are concerned, Muggles have been there, done

---

*Superconductivity is the very low electrical resistance exhibited by certain metals when cooled to a sufficiently low temperature.

that and bought the T-shirt. Archaeologists suspect that priestesses who occupied the sacred Oracle at Delphi, in Ancient Greece, saw visions because they inhaled natural gases such as ethane, ethylene and methane leaking from the limestone rocks below. The Greek historian who interpreted some of these visions, Plutarch, wrote of the sweet smells he experienced – a classic indicator of the presence of ethylene. In 1692, the witch trials in Salem, Massachusetts (see pages 12–14), followed a mysterious illness that stuck a number of girls, causing trances and hallucinations. One theory is that victims ate grain contaminated by a fungus called *ergot*, thought to contain hallucinogenic chemicals.

S IS FOR SNEAKOSCOPE
HOGWARTS VERSION

For his thirteenth birthday, Harry gets a pocket sneakoscope, a handy little device that lights up, whistles and spins when it detects someone untrustworthy close by. Sneakoscopes are a popular line at Dervish & Banges, the magical-supplies store based at Hogsmeade.

MUGGLES VERSION

Muggles do have a type of sneakoscope, although it's rather more cumbersome. Tests conducted by Honeywell Laboratories and the Mayo Clinic in Rochester, Minnesota, have established that blood flow increases around the eyes of a liar, producing increased heat that can then be picked up by a high-definition thermal camera. Researchers reckon the system is 80 per cent reliable – ten per cent better than a polygraph. One theory is that, in a stressful situation, such as lying, the body pumps blood around the eyes to improve their ability to spot a good escape route.

T IS FOR TIME TURNER
HOGWARTS VERSION

In order that Hermione could attend several lessons at the same time, Professor McGonagall gave her a time turner, a 'tiny sparkling hourglass' attached to a chain, one turn of which sends the holder back an hour in time. Hermione receives dire warnings from the professor about meddling in the past – specifically, the risk of killing a past self by mistake. Nonetheless, she and Harry successfully use it in a stunning caper.

MUGGLES VERSION

Oh my. We've been here before (see 'K', 'I' and 'D' above), but that won't stop your head hurting. In a nutshell, the general Muggle view on time travel is that there's nothing in Einstein's General Theory of Relativity that says you can't do it, it but that it's actually probably impossible to do. People like Professor Stephen Hawking – one of the relatively few people on the planet clever enough to grapple with time conundrums – point out that we have no reliable evidence of people from the future. However, others argue that this is because we haven't built a time machine yet and we can't go back beyond the point in history that we did. Or will.

One possible way of building a time machine, scientists currently believe, is to construct a wormhole (see under 'D'), transport one end of it vast distances through space at speeds close to the speed of light, and then return it to its original location, close to the other end of the wormhole.

This is where things get interesting. In his General Theory of Relativity, Einstein suggested the existence of a phenomenon known as *relativistic time dilation*, whereby time travels slower for objects travelling at close to light speed than it does in the normal universe. This means that someone in a spaceship travelling at such speeds will be rather upset at how old everyone has become on their return.

So what does this have to do with actual time travel? Well, in theory it means that, like our spaceship passenger, if you transport one end of a wormhole at such a huge velocity, it will be connected to a different point in time to the other end when it returns. A short hop through the wormhole should then, theoretically, transport you from one point in time to another. Funky, eh?

U IS FOR URANUS
HOGWARTS VERSION
Uranus jokes have been staple fare for fourth-formers since at least the 19th century, and so Ron Weasley was never going to miss his chance at Hogwarts. When, in the *Goblet Of Fire*, Professor Trelawney peers at Lavender Brown's star chart and informs her that her unaspected planet is Uranus, Ron quickly chips in, 'Can I have a look at Uranus, too, Lavender?' and they're all given extra homework. He's in hysterics about it once more in *Harry Potter And The Order Of The Phoenix*.

MUGGLES VERSION
Muggles who find themselves discussing Uranus over tea with the vicar should take care with pronunciation if they want to avoid embarrassment. Try practising in advance – *YER-un-us* – and then move quickly on to safer ground (metaphorically speaking) such as Neptune or Jupiter. For the record, Uranus is the seventh planet from the sun, orbits at a distance of some 2,870 million kilometres, has an atmosphere consisting mostly of hydrogen and helium and is the third largest planet in the Solar System in diameter. Most astronomers thought it was a star until William Herschel put them right in 1781.

V IS FOR VAMPIRE
HOGWARTS VERSION
Among Voldemort's nastier habits is a liking for blood – specifically, a few glasses of unicorn blood – to help him through the day. This suggests he may have a touch of vampire in his make-up, although it's also possible he's suffering from a disease called *porphyria*.

MUGGLES VERSION
The myths and legends surrounding vampires can be found elsewhere in these pages, but scientists have recently proposed a rational explanation for their activities. According to the Spanish neurologist Juan Gomez-Alonso, symptoms of vampirism such as insomnia, an aversion to mirrors and dislike of strong smells (such as garlic) are jolly similar to those endured by sufferers of rabies – which, of course, is spread by biting.

W IS FOR WHOMPING WILLOW
HOGWARTS VERSION
The Whomping Willow is a tree not to be tangled with, as generations of Hogwarts pupils can testify. It can sense – and wallop – any who approach its branches and jealously guards the entrance to one of the school's seven secret tunnels.

MUGGLES VERSION
The closest thing in the Muggle world to such aggressive plant-life is the formidable nepenthes vine, which grows upwards of 20m in length. It's effectively a giant version of the carnivorous Venus's fly-trap, with claw-like pods that trap flies. The flies land on trigger hairs on a pod, whereby the vine speedily transfers water from the pod's interior to exterior membranes, increasing pressure and forcing its trap shut. Nepenthes vines catch frogs, birds and even rats the same way. Don't stick your hand in.

X IS FOR X-RAY
HOGWARTS VERSION
In *Harry Potter And The Goblet Of Fire*, it is suggested that Professor Moody's magical eye possesses some X-ray qualities, because he can see straight through Harry's invisibility cloak. Dementors might have a similar ability to detect the presence of someone who's invisible, although it's possible that they simply sense someone nearby.

MUGGLES VERSION
Like all the neatest breakthroughs in Muggle science, X-rays were discovered by accident. In 1895, a German physicist named Wilhelm Roentgen sat in his

lab, firing electron beams down a gas discharge tube. He noticed that when he put his hand in front of the tube a silhouette of his bones appeared on a nearby fluorescent screen. This is one of those few occasions when a Muggle boffin simultaneously discovers something and then immediately spots the most useful way to use it (ie in medicine)! X-rays are similar to visible light rays – ie they are waveforms of electromagnetic energy – but they possess higher energy and so can pass through, say, your body. Soft tissues don't absorb the rays well, but bones do, which is why they show up clearly on X-ray negatives. As for X-ray vision…well, that scientific happy accident has yet to happen, but never say never.

Y IS FOR YETI
HOGWARTS VERSION
Yeti are giant, furry, ape-like beasts that live in the Himalayas and ferociously assault anyone who crosses their path. Professor Lockhart boasted about how he once cured one of a bad head cold. Hmm.

MUGGLES VERSION
Yeti are probably mythical creatures, and are also known in various parts of the Muggle world as Abominable Snowmen, while they have cousins in similar-looking (and similarly elusive) beasts Rakshasa, Bigfoot and Sasquatch. The most famous piece of Sasquatch evidence is some home-movie footage shot by Roger Patterson in Bluff Creek, California, in 1967. Sceptics believe this actually shows someone tramping around the forest in a specially made ape suit. Even so, would *you* have volunteered to go and check?

Z IS FOR ZOMBIE
HOGWARTS VERSION
Although not actually referred to as 'zombies' it's pretty clear that Inferi have a lot in common with these monsters. They're portrayed as the living dead and are like zombies, being trained and enslaved by Voldemort, much like a circus lion is trained to do tricks. Zombies do get the odd reference in Harry's adventures, however; Professor Quirrel is supposed to have been given a turban by an African prince in reward for chasing off a troublesome one.

MUGGLES VERSION
Some reports suggest that up to 1,000 cases of zombification are reported each year on Haiti, the spiritual home of the Voodoo religion. Doctors believe that the condition may be induced by a powerful neurotoxin called *tetrodotoxin*, obtained from porcupines and puffer fish and found in the 'zombification powder' used by Voodoo sorcerers, known as *bokos*. It's thought that bokos paralyse their victims so effectively with this powder that they appear to be

dead. Later these helpless, half-dead creatures are told the sorcerer has removed their soul, or *zombi astral*, and that they have no independent will. The effects of the neurotoxin mimic those of the Imperius curse, and this psychological device seems enough to consign some to lives of slavery.

AND FINALLY...

Since we started with a quote, we might as well finish with one. As science-fiction writer Arthur C Clarke once pointed out, 'Any sufficiently advanced technology is indistinguishable from magic.' That could have been Dumbledore talking!

— WIZARD TRANSPORT —

You might expect wizards and witches to be restricted in their means of transport to the humble broomstick, but Harry, his friends, their families and Hogwarts teachers all use different methods of getting about, the majority of which are swifter and more efficient than anything on offer to us Muggles. Here's a guide to how wizards travel.

HOGWARTS EXPRESS

The *Hogwarts Express* is one of the enduring features of the Harry Potter series. Readers can almost hear its whistle screech and taste its sooty clouds of smoke when Harry and the others set off for school. It's also a quick way to root the story in fantasy land, as steam trains haven't been used on British main lines since August 1968.

Although such trains are fondly remembered by those who grew up in the age of steam, they were messy things. On average they ate 60lb of coal per mile and drank some 75 gallons of water for that same short distance. They operated on the principle that water that has undergone sufficient heating (ie boiling) generates intense pressure. The steam that such heating produced was piped into cylinders and used to push pistons back and forth. These pistons worked an arrangement of crankshafts and connecting rods that ultimately turned the wheels.

The fastest recorded steam train was the *Mallard*, which achieved 126mph (202kph) on 3 July 1938. That compares pretty poorly with the fastest diesel train, which on 1 November 1967 was recorded as travelling at 148mph (237kph), or the speedy TGV electric train in France that set a 322mph (515.3kph) record in France on 8 May 1990.

Actually, most steam engines weren't scarlet, like the *Hogwarts Express*, but green or black, because those colours were less likely to show the smuts. The most famous steam train in the UK is actually not the *Hogwarts Express* but the *Flying Scotsman*, last used in 1963 and recently restored at a cost of £750,000 on behalf of the National Railway Museum in York. Although in the West steam travel is today largely restricted to tourist attractions, steam locomotives are still occasionally built in China.

We don't know how long the line between King's Cross and Hogwarts runs, but it's likely to be only a fraction of the distance of the world's longest railway, the Trans-Siberian Railway, which stretches for 5,800 miles (9,335km) between Moscow and Vladivostock. The journey from one end to the other takes some three weeks to complete.

However, regular rail users might view with envy the apparent punctuality of the *Hogwarts Express*, which many judge to be another, more significant indicator of the train being fictitious rather than real! In 2003, only four out of every five rail journeys in the UK started and finished on time. One estimate says that Britain's railway passengers wasted a total 4,632 years during 2001 as a result of late trains.

APPARATING/DISAPPARATING
The Ministry of Magic has imposed age restrictions on apparating, which no one under the age of 17 is permitted to do. Longstanding charms make it impossible to apparate or disapparate within the grounds of Hogwarts school. (Just imagine the chaos that would ensue if pupils could appear and disappear at will during classes!)

HORSE-DRAWN CARRIAGE
Beauxbatons staff and pupils travel to Hogwarts in a giant carriage drawn by winged palomino-like horses the size of elephants that drink only single-malt whisky.

SHIP
Durmstrang students arrive at Hogwarts in a ghostly vessel that can travel underwater. The ship is reminiscent of the *Flying Dutchman*, which in the 17th century was supposedly condemned by the curse of its captain to sail forever the waters around the Cape of Good Hope, the southern tip of Africa. Just as Hogwarts' students were spellbound by the Durmstrang ship's portal lights, so witnesses of the *Flying Dutchman* have been hypnotised by swing lamps along the yard arm.

BOAT
Hagrid takes first-year pupils arriving at Hogwarts across the lake on a boat ostensibly powered by sail, despite the apparent threat of menace from the resident giant squid that lives there. When Dennis Creevey falls into the lake in *Harry Potter And The Goblet Of Fire*, it is thought that the giant squid possibly pushed him back into the boat. It is also Hagrid who transports Harry from the Hut-on-the-Rock in *Harry Potter And The Philosopher's Stone* in a boat, which he powers with two brisk taps from a pink umbrella.

BROOMSTICKS
To most children it's a witches' broom, but actually the garden tool that ferries Harry and friends around is properly called a *besom broom*, and it has a long and proud history.

This kind of broom has been used for centuries both in and outside the home. In some parts of the country, heather was once used for the brush, as it was both plentiful and effective, although traditionally birch wood is used. The besom broom industry once centred on the Hampshire village of Tadley, where birch grows like a garden weed, so when the people at Warner Bros were looking for brooms to feature in their production of *Harry Potter And The Goblet Of Fire*, they visited Tadley to call on the services of the Arthur Nash Broom Company.

Sadly, Arthur Nash, whose family has been making brooms for three centuries, died shortly before the film studio's order for 84 brooms was placed. However, the business is being continued by his son, Bradley, his son-in-law, Andrew Taylor, and his daughters, Amanda and Lisa, who together produced the necessary props, which were used during the Quidditch World Cup scene. The company also supplies brooms for the Queen (they have a royal warrant to prove it) as well as the Museum of Witchcraft in Cornwall and the general public.

Although it takes only about five minutes to put a broom together, it is a year before all the components are ready for use. Arthur's widow, Sue, explains: 'The birch is cut between November and March, when there is no sap and no leaves. Then it is stacked and pressed for six months. Afterwards, each branch is picked by hand, when the branches are pulled apart.' Only after being stored for a further six months is the wood ready for use.

Hazel branches are generally used for broom handles, and these have to be cut and shaved twice before they are ready. The brush was originally held in place with wire, but after the 17th century supple willow bonds were used instead to save on expense. Following the Second World War, wire came to be used exclusively, and the art of making bonds is now almost forgotten.

The only differences between the brooms ordered by Warner Bros and regular brooms were that those used in the film had brushes that were left bushy, and the bark remained on the wood, to be used as handgrips.

That long-established tradition of witches on broomsticks began, as we know now, through lax security at early Quidditch matches, which has since been remedied by the Department of Magical Games and Sports.

A broad choice of broomstick has been available to wizards over the years for the purposes of playing Quidditch. After the crude beginnings of the Oakshaft 79, there came the Moontrimmer, the Cleansweep 1 (the first of a series extending to the Cleansweep 11), the Bluebottle, the Comet series and the

Tinderblast, with its Art Deco influences, which emerged in 1940. Afterwards came the Shooting Star, the Nimbus 1000, the Nimbus 2000, the Nimbus 2001, a selection of Silver Arrows, the Twigger 90 (prone to warping) and the top-of-the-range Firebolt, as used by our hero.

PORTKEY

An unobtrusive object used by wizard for swift transportation, the portkey's great asset is that Muggles never suspect the immense power possessed by such an apparently mundane item. Travelling via portkey is also brilliantly quick but can be very unexpected, which brings with it hidden dangers, as Harry and Cedric discover in *Harry Potter And The Goblet Of Fire*.

FLYING CARS

Strictly speaking, the car is a Muggle object, but with his love of all things Muggle, Arthur Weasley couldn't resist transforming a standard mode of transport into something that's strictly for wizards.

The flying car that transports Ron and Harry to Hogwarts is instantly recognisable by its sleek lines. The Ford Anglia 105E – once a familiar sight on British roads – is now rarely seen. It first rolled off the production lines in 1959, the same year as the Mini, and was the third in a series of Anglias with a modest price tag for the standard model of £589. Heavily influenced by the lines of popular American cars of the era, with bug-eye headlamps, swept-back nose, tailfins and a backward-slanting rear window, the Ford Anglia 105E was nonetheless dramatically different to anything else around on the roads at the time. When it was launched, on 30 September that year, a press release by the manufacturers promised, 'Ford's bold approach to design has resulted in a vehicle that is new in every detail: styling, engine, transmission, suspension and furnishing.

'From the likes, dislikes, preferences and prejudices of thousands of potential customers in nine countries, the company's design team has created a car that is as near to the image of public demand as market study and experience can make it. And by a brutal half-million-mile testing programme covering four continents, they have produced what is unquestionably the most thoroughly researched and exhaustively tested light car the world has ever seen.'

Production of the car continued at the Halewood plant in Dagenham until 1967, during which time about 954,000 were made and after which it made way for the Ford Escort Mark I, which first appeared in 1968. JK Rowling included the car in her book not only because it was so charmingly distinctive but also because she and a pal used to ride around in one. 'My heart still lifts when I see an old Ford Anglia,' she once confessed.

There are a couple of crucial differences between an on-the-road Ford Anglia and the car that appears in the Harry Potter book and film, of course. If you're lucky enough to come by one, don't expect it to stretch magically so that it can accommodate a large family; four is about the maximum number of people you can comfortably fit in one. It's also unlikely to become invisible, unless car thieves have passed by. Although it is aerodynamically designed, the chances of it getting off the ground at all are also pretty remote, and trying to make it fly is certainly something you shouldn't try without the supervision of a wizard.

ENCHANTED CARS
Using his influence at the Ministry of Magic, Arthur Weasley secures the services of two cars to transport the children to King's Cross from the Burrow at the start of *Harry Potter And The Prisoner Of Azkaban*. These were much like ordinary cars in most respects, although they did display the ability to squeeze through unfeasibly small gaps on the road. At the wheel of each was a wizard driver.

MOTORBIKE
The airborne motorbike is the transport of choice for Sirius Black, who obviously rates it as a reliable and safe way of getting about as he lends the enchanted two-wheeler to Hagrid to help secure the safety of the infant Harry. On Muggle roads, the motorbike safety record is far less impressive, with numerous motorcyclists coming to grief each year.

KNIGHT BUS
The Knight Bus, which picks up Harry for a hair-raising ride in *Harry Potter And The Prisoner Of Azkaban*, was specially constructed for the makers of the film version by welding together two Routemaster buses, the red double-deckers that for decades have trundled along London's streets. As each bus was almost half a century old, there were certain modifications that needed to be made before the construct could be captured on camera. For instance, the cabin was moved closer to the front, while inside curtains and chandeliers were installed, along with a generator to power the extra lights. Both upper decks were detachable, and during filming they were transported on the back of a lorry.

In Harry's world, the Knight Bus can comfortably achieve speeds in excess of 65mph, but in the film it went no faster than 35mph, while the cars coming towards it were travelling at a sedate 10mph. Fancy film work did the rest. Still, no fewer than 30 stunt drivers were used during the filming of the scene, and not all the takes were used for the movie. One night, filming was interrupted when a stolen Range Rover sped past the £160,000 Knight Bus down a road specially closed for the movie-makers, with the police in hot pursuit.

FLYING CARPETS

Although they are the height of style in some magical environments, flying carpets have never achieved popularity in the wizarding world inhabited by Harry Potter, mainly because of the carpet's close associations with the Muggle world. In fact, there's a wizard prohibition order in place to prevent carpets from being charmed for the purpose of airborne travel. However, this doesn't stop Ali Bashir trying to make a fast galleon by selling some.

HIPPOGRIFF

A Hippogriff is a curious-looking creature with the head, wings and front legs of a griffin while its hindquarters are all horse. In addition to the Harry Potter series, Hippogriffs feature in several epic poems written years ago, as well as in Greek art, where they're used as a symbol of love. This is perhaps because griffins and horses are supposed to loathe one another, so the coupling that produced the Hippogriff must have been an against-all-odds romance. Sirius Black travels by Hippogriff after going on the run, and as the Hippogriff prefers to fly at high altitudes, it must have been a breathtaking series of rides for Sirius, in more ways than one.

THESTRALS

These striking if somewhat ugly winged horses dwell in the Forbidden Forest and pull the carriages ferrying Hogwarts pupils from Hogsmeade Station to the school at the start of term. Sometimes thestrals are invisible to the naked eye, although they have always been apparent to some pupils. Harry sees them for the first time in *Harry Potter And The Order Of The Phoenix*.

FLOO POWDER

An ingenious system of travel, but not for the faint-hearted. In effect, using Floo powder requires you to step into a fire to travel or place your head into the flames to send a message. It works like this: you deliver a generous pinch of sparkly Floo powder to the fire and state your destination. (The Floo powder has the happy effect of making a blazing fire feel like nothing more than blasts of warm air.) Then, trusting to magic, it's time to jump into the fire and be transported at breathtaking speed to the fireplace of your choice. Travelling via the Floo network isn't a sensation Harry enjoys, but it's frequently used by the Weasley family, among others, to get from A to B. Harry has also used Floo powder to talk to Sirius, whose head bobbed about in the flames at Grimmauld Place in a kind of wizarding equivalent to video phones. Needless to say, such a mode of travel should never be tried by a Muggle with a domestic fireplace. It won't work and it's extremely dangerous.

— HARRY POTTER GAZETEER —

Alnwick Castle in Northumberland was the location for some Quidditch matches and broomstick-flying lessons in the Harry Potter films. Fittingly, the castle also boasts a spellbinding new addition: Britain's first Poison Garden. In 2004, then-Home Secretary David Blunkett granted the Alnwick Garden Trust a special licence that permitted the growth of cannabis, magic mushrooms, opium poppies and a further 50 'dangerous' plants. A Home Office spokesman said, 'It is extremely rare for these sorts of licences to be granted, and they are only granted for education or research purposes, if it is in the public interest to do so.'

Black Park, Langley, Berkshire, was used for shots of the Forbidden Forest during the Harry Potter films, looking a world away from Heathrow Airport, which is spookily close.

Blackpool Pier is where Neville's great-uncle wanted to test him for hitherto unseen magical prowess by tossing him in the sea.

The Bodleian Library at Oxford University appears in the film *Harry Potter And The Goblet Of Fire.* Other parts of the university have been used for filming, including the 15th-century Divinity School, which has doubled as the Hogwarts hospital wing.

Borough Market, London, became the exterior of the Leaky Cauldron in *Harry Potter And The Prisoner Of Azkaban.*

Chipping Sodbury, Gloucestershire, is where JK Rowling was born.

Christ Church, Oxford, doubles as the Hogwarts dining hall.

Durham Cathedral's cloisters appear in the Harry Potter films, and the Transfiguration class was filmed there. It's also where the scenes set in Moaning Myrtle's toilet were shot.

Exeter University is where JK Rowling graduated with a degree in French.

Exmoor is the backdrop for many of the outdoor scenes in *Harry Potter And The Goblet Of Fire.*

Glencoe, Scotland, is where filming for *Harry Potter And The Goblet Of Fire* began on 22 March 2004. For many of the cast and crew, this was a return visit, as filming also took place there for *Harry Potter And The Prisoner Of Azkaban*, as it was where Hagrid's hut was sited.

Gloucester Cathedral's cloisters have become Hogwarts corridors, as can be seen in *Harry Potter And The Philosopher's Stone* when Snape quizzes Quirrel. Pupils from the nearby King's School appear as extras in this scene.

Goathland Station in North Yorkshire is the perfect double for Hogsmeade Station. If you think it looks familiar, it's because the station and nearby village have regularly appeared in the ITV 1950s drama *Heartbeat*.

King's Cross Station is a famous London rail terminal that's also the setting for departures for Hogwarts. Be warned, though, that platform $9^3/_4$ doesn't really exist, and no amount of crashing luggage trolleys into station walls will get you onto the *Hogwarts Express*. However, look out for a sign indicating its existence, put up by railway authorities to satisfy scores of sightseers who flocked to the station to see the launch point of Harry's Hogwarts career.

Lacock Abbey in Wiltshire, which dates from the 13th century, has become familiar territory to Harry Potter fans, as it is often used for Hogwarts shots.

Leavesden Studios, Watford, is where all the studio scenes for *Harry Potter And The Prisoner Of Azkaban* were shot. A Quidditch grandstand, the Quidditch World Cup camp site and a dragon's lair have also been built there for the *Harry Potter And The Goblet Of Fire* film.

London Zoo is where the scene was shot in which Harry first learns that he can speak parseltongue and communicate with snakes.

Nicholls Lane, Winterbourne, is the address of JK Rowling's childhood home.

Nicolson's Restaurant, Edinburgh, while now a Chinese restaurant, was once a café, and when JK Rowling's daughter was asleep in a pushchair, this is where the aspiring author would park herself to write reams in longhand.

Palmer's Green, London, is the suburban setting for the Knight Bus rides.

Peebles is the home of Angus Fleet, a Muggle who reported seeing the flying Ford Anglia in action, thus confirming the suspicion that Hogwarts lies in northern Scotland.

Picket Post Close, Martin's Heron, Bracknell, Berkshire, is the location used as Privet Drive, home of the dreadful Dursleys, in the first two Harry Potter movies.

The Royal Albert Hall is where JK Rowling was interviewed by Stephen Fry in front of 4,500 students on 26 June 2003. Hundreds more watched online as she completed the day by reading from her then-latest book, *Harry Potter And The Order Of The Phoenix.*

Shepperton Studios, Middlesex, is where numerous films have been made in the last 50 years or so. It's here that the lake scenes at the end of *Harry Potter And The Prisoner Of Azkaban* were filmed.

St Pancras Station is a grand neighbour of King's Cross, and its grand façade can be seen in the Harry Potter films when the Hogwarts pupils go to meet their school train.

Sunridge Park, Yate, is another home address for JK Rowling during her childhood.

Tutshill, Gloucestershire, is where JK Rowling grew up.

Virginia Water, Surrey, is an oasis of peace in the vicinity of some major roads, and it's where some of the Care of Magical Creatures class scenes were filmed in the Harry Potter films.

Wyedean Comprehensive, Sedbury, is the secondary school at which JK Rowling became Head Girl.

— INDEX —